# THE BES
# OLD LANCASHIRE
## IN POETRY AND VERSE

Selected and Edited
by
Cliff Hayes

PRINTWISE PUBLICATIONS LIMITED
1992

This Edition
© Printwise Publications Ltd 1992

Published by Printwise Publications Ltd
47 Bradshaw Road, Tottington, Bury, Lancs, BL8 3PW.

Warehouse and Orders:
40-42 Willan Industrial Estate, Vere Street,
(off Eccles New Road),
Salford, M5 2GR.
Tel: 061-745 9168 Fax: 061-737 1755

Most of the text comes from *Modern Songs & Ballads of Lancashire* edited by JOHN HARLAND F.S.A in 1866.

ISBN No. 1 872226 50 7

Re-edited and page design by

All rights reserved

No part of this publication may be reproduced, stored in a retrieval system or transmitted in any form or by any means, electronic, mechanical, photocopying, recording or otherwise without the prior permission of the publisher.

Printed and bound by Manchester Free Press,
Paragon Mill, Jersey Street,
Manchester, M4 6FP
Tel: 061-236 8822

# INTRODUCTION

The title of this book may seem a bit odd in that Lancashire does not seem to be a place to inspire poetry. But this is not the case. There is a fine tradition of poetry and song in Lancashire, some in dialect and some in straight English.

It has been a labour of love for me searching for these gems of Lancashire's literary past. Most of the works in this book are taken from a book called *Modern Songs and Ballads of Lancashire* edited by John Harland F.S.A. in 1866. John Harland collected poems and verse from around Lancashire. Some were published in newspapers, or periodicals, some were from professional poets, some from pure amateurs. He also collected fascinating facts about the lives of the authors where known, and produced a very enjoyable book that I am sure will interest and entertain readers of today.

Some of the original poems did not travel the 140 years well, and have been replaced with others that were written after this book was first published, poems by Ben Brierly for instance.

I feel that the selection here is the collected talents of the cream of the last century. Mrs Linneaus Banks (famous for the *Manchester Man*) wrote gentle poetry that is aiso included. Mrs Heman, famous for her 'boy stood on the burning deck', is well represented and many others, that we hope you will enjoy.

I hope that you agree with me that these poets and their works deserve a new lease of life, and that you get from them the same enjoyment that they gave when first created.

## TAKEN FROM THE ORIGINAL PREFACE

The pleasurable duty remains of thanking all those to whom, far more than to the Editor, this volume owes its existence. He has merely gathered the flowers of Lancashire song into a garland. Theirs is the fragrance of these poetic blossoms; theirs the rich and varied tints that delight the eye. To thank each individually by name would be simply to repeat the table of contents; and ·he can therefore only tender to one and all, his most grateful thanks for the courteous and ready kindness with which they have acceded to his request. To the surviving representatives of deceased writers, and to various publishing firms holding copyrights, he must take leave, in like manner, to tender his sincere acknowledgments.

SWINTON, *October* 1865.

JOHN HARLAND F.R.S.

# LANCASHIRE LYRICS:

## MODERN
## *SONGS AND BALLADS*

OF THE

## COUNTY PALATINE.

EDITED BY

### JOHN HARLAND, F.S.A.,

EDITOR OF "BALLADS AND SONGS OF LANCASHIRE, CHIEFLY OLDER THAN THE NINETEENTH CENTURY."

· LONDON:
WHITTAKER & CO., AVE MARIA LANE.
1866.

# ACKNOWLEDGEMENTS

Thanks must go to the second-hand bookshops who put up with my digging and delving and their help in collecting together old leaflets, postcards and books on Manchester. Special mention to Jimmy McGill on Princess Road (well worth a browse) and not forgettting Harry; Tony Gibb in Charlotte Street, and the young whipper-snapper Rob; Alan Seddon from Browzers in Prestwich; Brian Barlow in Beech Road, Chorlton; John from Fennel Books in the Corn Exchange; Harry from Heaton's Bookshop in Heaton Mersey; George Kelsall in Littleborough, and many others.

Thanks lads.

## DEDICATED

To Father David Ryder
Hospital Chaplain to Withington and
Christie Hospitals, Manchester.

# CONTENTS

## 1 ROMANTIC AND LEGENDARY BALLADS

| | | |
|---|---|---|
| THE EVE OF ST JOHN | *Charles Swain* | 11 |
| THE WILD RIDER | *Samuel Bamford* | 14 |
| A LEGEND OF THE HEART | *John Bolton Rogerson* | 22 |
| BALLAD | *Charles Swain* | 25 |
| THE MANDRAKE | *William Harrison Ainsworth* | 26 |
| THE HUNTER'S SONG | *Rev. Richard Pakinson, D.D* | 28 |
| A BALLAD | *Charles Swain* | 31 |
| CLAYTON HALL | *Elijah Ridings* | 32 |
| THE WANDERER | *Charles Swain* | 34 |
| THE BILLMEN OF BOWLAND | *From "Ned of the fell"* | 37 |
| BLACK BESS | *William Harrison Ainsworth* | 38 |
| GYPSY BALLAD | *Charles Swain* | 41 |
| OLD GRINDROD'S GHOST | *William Harrison Ainsworth* | 42 |
| THE KEEPERS SON | *R.R. Bealey* | 45 |
| THE BALLAD OF JAMES AND JANE | *Henry Kirk* | 47 |
| DERWENTWATER'S FATE | *Anonymous* | 50 |

## II LOVE SONGS AND PRAISES OF THE FAIR

| | | |
|---|---|---|
| LOVE EVIL CHOICE | *Mrs Habergham* | 53 |
| THE SPRIG OF THYME | *From the Greaves Collecton* | 55 |
| COLIN AND PHEBE | *John Byrom* | 56 |
| SONGS | *William Rowlinson of Manchester* | 59 |
| MARGARET | *ditto* | 60 |
| REMEMBER ME | *ditto* | 61 |
| THE INVITATION | *ditto* | 62 |
| KITTY AN' ROBIN | *Auther of "Scarsdale"* | 63 |
| MEG OR JENNY? | *ditto* | 64 |
| OH, WELL I LOVE MY GENTILE MAID | *J.B. Rogerson* | 65 |
| THE LOVER'S CALL | *J.C. Prince* | 67 |
| MY WYNDER | *Samuel Bamford* | 68 |
| CANZONETTE | *J.B. Rogerson* | 70 |
| SHE'S NOT SO FAIR | *Charles Swain* | 71 |
| MY JOHNNY | *R.R. Bealey* | 72 |
| BERTHA | *Henry Kirk of Goosnargh* | 73 |
| TO MARY | *John Harland F.R.S* | 74 |

| | | |
|---|---|---|
| COME, LOVE AND SING | J.B. Rogerson | 75 |
| SERENADE | William Mort | 76 |
| WE MET | Henry Kirk | 77 |
| I'LL TELL MY MOTHER | J.B. Rogerson | 78 |
| TH' SWEETHEART GATE | Edwin Waugh | 79 |
| THE LOVED AND LOST | Henry Kirk | 80 |
| LOVELY SUSANNAH | Thomas Nicholson | 81 |
| MAGGIE | Richard R. Bealey | 82 |
| BETTER THAN BEAUTY | Charles Swain | 83 |
| NOTHING MORE | John Bolton Rogerson | 84 |
| NUPTIAL LINES | George Richarson | 85 |
| "I GAZED O'ER THE BLUE STILL WATERS" | James Horton Groves | 86 |
| BUT I AM SAD | R.R. Bealey | 87 |
| "OH, MIRK AND STORMY" | James Horton Groves | 88 |
| "IN A SNUG LITTLE NOOK" | Thomas Brierley | 90 |
| THE ARDENT LOVER | The Late, Edward Rushton, of Liverpool | 91 |
| THE LANCASHIRE WITCH | The Late John Scholes | 92 |
| TH' HEART-BROKKEN | John Higson, of Droylesden | 94 |
| THE DOMINIE'S COURTSHIP | Robert Rockliff | 95 |
| BERTHA | Henry Kirk | 96 |

## III  SONGS OF HOME AND ITS AFFECTIONS

| | | |
|---|---|---|
| IT IS BUT A COTTAGE | Charles Swain | 97 |
| THE PLEASURE O'WHOAM | Joseph Ramsbottom | 98 |
| FAREWELL TO MY COTTAGE | Samuel Bamford | 99 |
| EARLY HAUNTS VISITED | R.W. Procter | 101 |
| HOME | Charles Swain | 102 |
| THE MUSIC IN OUR HOME | Mrs WM Hobson | 103 |
| THE SONGS OF OUR FATHER | Mrs Hemans | 104 |
| DOMESTIC MELODY | J.C.Prince | 106 |
| HOME AND FRIENDS | Charles Swain | 107 |
| MINE! (A Wife's Song) | Mrs.G. Linnaeus Banks | 108 |
| EDITH | R.R. Bealy | 109 |
| "AS WELCOME AS FLOWERS IN MAY" | J.C. Prince | 110 |
| THE POET TO HIS WIFE | William Mort | 112 |
| THE STAR OF THE HOUSEHOLD | John Critchley Prince | 114 |
| "TIS SWEET TO MEET THE FRIEND WE LOVE" | George Richardson | 116 |
| WELCOME, BONNY BIRD! | Samuel Laycock | 117 |
| THE LOST BROTHER | William Mort | 119 |
| EVENING SONG | J.C. Prince | 120 |

| | | |
|---|---|---|
| LOVED AND LOST | Mrs Trafford Whitehead | 122 |
| EAWR BESSY | Richard R. Bealey | 124 |
| THE CHILD AND THE DEWDROPS | J.C. Prince | 127 |
| TO LITTLE ANGEL "CHARLIE" | R.R. Bealy | 128 |
| THE LAST BEHEST | William Mort | 130 |
| "GOD BLESS THESE POOR WIMMEN THAT'S CHILDER!" | Thomas Brierley | 132 |
| THE KISS BENEATH THE HOLLY | Mrs William Hobson | 133 |
| MI GRONFEYTHER | Samuel Laycock | 134 |
| LINES TO MY WIFE | Samuel Bamford | 136 |
| ANGEL ANNIE | Mrs William Hobson | 138 |
| MY IDEAL HOME | ditto | 140 |

## IV  SONGS OF LIFE AND BROTHERHOOD

| | | |
|---|---|---|
| THE SONGS OF THE PEOPLE | John Critchley Prince | 142 |
| "WHY, PHITHEE NOW" | John Byrom | 143 |
| THE CHILD | Late John Briggs | 144 |
| "THERE'S NO CHAP SHOULD EVER LOSE PLUCK." | Richard R. Bealey | 145 |
| THE GARLAND OF LIFE | The Late J.B. Rogerson | 146 |
| TOPER'S PLEA FOR DRINKING | The Late Rev. Thamas Wilson B.D | 148 |
| "HEAW QUARE IS THIS LOIFE!" | Thomas Brierley | 149 |
| HUMAN BROTHERHOOD | John Critchley Prince | 150 |
| THE GOOD SPIRIT | Mrs.G. Linnaeus Banks | 151 |
| THE SUN AND THE FLOWERS | James Watson "The Doctor" | 152 |
| SONG OF THE EXILE | The Late Rev. Richard Parkinson D.D. | 153 |
| THINK NOT OF FAILURE | Mrs W.M. Hobson | 154 |
| A WELCOME | James Dawson, Jon | 155 |
| AVARICE | The Late Rev. Thomas Wilson | 156 |
| LINES WRITTEN IN A BOAT | The Late Rev. Richard Parkinson | 157 |
| THE WEAVER OF WELLBROOK | B.Brierley | 158 |
| THE LESSON OF THE LEAVES | Mrs .G. Linnaeus Banks | 159 |
| "MY PIECE ISOBU' WOVEN EAWT" | Richard R. Bealey | 160 |
| HOPE AND PERSEVERANCE | John Critchley Prince | 161 |
| OUR DAILY PATHS | Mrs Hemans | 162 |
| DO A TURN WHEN YOU CAN | Charles Swain | 164 |
| HELP ONE ANOTHER | Thomas Brierley | 165 |
| THE SONG OF OTHER DAYS | Robert Rockliff | 166 |
| SONG OF THE PEOPLE | William Mort | 167 |
| WELCOME WHITSUNTIDE | Mrs W.M. Hobson | 169 |
| BE KIND TO EACH OTHER | Charles Swain | 171 |
| FAREWELL | The Late John Just | 172 |
| STANZAS WRITTEN TO MUSIC | The Late Rev. Richard Parkinson | 173 |

| | | |
|---|---|---|
| FRIENDS DO NOT DIE | Richard R. Bealey | 174 |
| KINDLY WORDS | J.C. Prince | 175 |
| ENGLANDS DEAD | Mrs Hemans | 176 |
| SONGS FOR THE BRAVE | Samuel Bamford | 178 |
| FAME | Thomas Brierley | 179 |
| THE TRIED AND TRUE | Mrs George Linnaeus Banks | 180 |
| THE PASS OF DEATH | Samuel Bamford | 181 |
| FINIS | Charles Swain | 183 |

## V  LAYS OF THE COTTON FAMINE

| | | |
|---|---|---|
| THE MILL-HANDS PETITION | From a Broadside | 184 |
| THE FACTORY LASS | Joseph Ramsbottom | 185 |
| "SHORT TIME, COME AGAIN ON MORE." | From a Broadside | 186 |
| THE SMOKELESS CHIMNEY | by a Lancashire Lady | 187 |
| "GOD BLESS 'EM, IT SHOWS THEY'N SOME THOWT!" | Samuel Laycock | 189 |
| "CHEER UP A BIT LONGER." | Samuel Laycock | 191 |
| FRETTIN! | Joseph Ramsbottom | 192 |
| TH' SHURAT WEAVER'S SONG | Samuel Laycock | 193 |
| GOOIN' T' SCHOO' | Joseph Ramsbottom | 195 |
| HARD TIMES: OR, TH' WEYVUR TO HIS WIFE | A Lancshire Lad (James Bowker) | 197 |

## VI  SEA SONGS

| | | |
|---|---|---|
| WILL CLEWLINE | The Late Edward Rushton | 199 |
| ABSENCE | ditto | 202 |
| THE NEGLECTED TAR | ditto | 203 |
| THE LASS OF LIVERPOOL | ditto | 205 |
| "WHEN THE BROAD ARCH OF HEAVEN" | ditto | 206 |
| THE FAREWELL | ditto | 208 |
| CASABIANCA | Mrs F. Hemans | 210 |
| A THOUGHT OF THE SEA | ditto | 211 |
| DISTANT SOUND OF THE SEA AT EVENING | ditto | 211 |

FINIS

## I.

## Romantic and Legendary Ballads.

### THE EVE OF ST JOHN:

#### By Charles Swain.

She waiteth by the forest stream,
　　She sitteth on the ground;
While the moonlight, like a mantle,
　　Wraps her tenderly around!
She sitteth through the cold, cold night,
　　But not a step draws near;
Though *his* name is on her trembling lips,
　　His voice meets not her ear!

Hist! was 't the haunted stream that spoke?
　　What droning sound swept there?
She listens!—Still no human tone
　　O'erhears she anywhere!
Oh! was 't the forest bough that took
　　That sad and spectral mien?
She looketh round distractedly,
　　But there is nothing seen!

Dark, in the quiet moonlight,
   Her shadowy form is thrown;
With a strange and lonely mournfulness,
   *It seems not like her own!*
She glanceth o'er her shoulder fair,
   The moon is gleaming wide;
She turneth—Jesu! what is there
   Pale sitting by her side?

She pauseth for a single breath—
   She hearkens for a tone;
And terror pains her chilling veins,
   For breath or sound is none!
The silence—oh! it racks her brain,
   It binds it like a cord;
She'd given worlds, though but to hear
   The chirping of a bird.

The shadow rose before her,
   It stood upon the stream:
" O blessed shadow, ease my soul,
   And tell me 'tis a dream!
Thou tak'st the form of one they vow'd
   Mine eyes should see no more!"
The shadow stood across the stream,
   And beckon'd pale before.

The shadow beckon'd on before,
   Yet deign'd her no reply;
The lady rose, and straight the stream
   To its pebbly breast was dry.
It pass'd the wood, it cross'd the court,
   The gate flew from its chain;
The gentle ladye knew she stood
   Within her own domain!

And still the awful shadow glid,
   Without or breath or tone,
Until it came to a sullen sluice,
   'Mid yellow sand and stone;
But rock and sand disdain'd to stand,
   The water scorn'd to flow;
Thus blood was seen down the rift between,
   And the dead reveal'd below.

The dead was seen, in the space between,
  And the ladye knew it well!
She kiss'd its cheek, with a piercing shriek,
  With a woe no tongue may tell.
The gory shadow beckon'd on,
  And still her steps implored;
But she follow'd not, for on that spot
  She found a shiver'd sword.


She grasp'd the hilt, its silken thread
  Her own fair skill had wove;
A brother's hand had struck the dead—
  *His* sword had slain her love!
She took the corpse upon her knees,
  Its cheek lay next her own;
Like sculpture fair, in the moonlight there,
  Like misery turn'd to stone!

  .    .    .    .    .    .

No food to seek for the ravens' beak,
  The gibbet serves them true,
With young and sweet and dainty meat,
  As e'er the ravens knew;
And few they see near the gibbet tree,
  For a bleeding form glides on,
From the haunted stream, in the moon's cold beam
  On the eve of good Saint John!

## THE WILD RIDER.

### (A LEGENDARY TALE.)

### BY SAMUEL BAMFORD.

#### PART FIRST.

Now unto fair Alkrington tidings there came,
And the gallant young knight he soon heard of the same,
That a gentle young damsel had passèd that morn,
And was gone up a hunting with hound and with horn;
"And oh!" said Sir Ashton, " if that be the case,
Methinks I would fain join the maid in the chase,
And so bid my groom-boy, withouten delay,
Bring forth my white hunter, I'll ride her to-day."

And soon his white hunter was led to the gate,
Where, neighing and pacing, she scarcely would wait;
She champ'd the steel bit, and she flung her head high,
As if she would fain snuff the air of the sky,
And wist not to breathe the low wind of the plain,
Which spread like a white cloud her tail and her mane;
"And oh!" thought the knight, as he view'd her with pride,
"The game should be love when my Arab I ride."

The knight he rode south, over Blakeley's high land,
But tidings he heard not of maid or her band;
The knight he rode east, towards the uprising sun,
But the broad heaths of Moston lay silent and dun;
And then he sped north, but she did not appear;
The cry of the hunter came not to his ear,
Till o'er lonely Syddall awoke a far strain,
And he rode till he join'd the fair maid and her train.

And who was the maiden that, plumed so gay,
Went forth with the hounds and good hunters that day?
And why did the damsel make slight of all heed,
Or whither she went with her hound and her steed?
And why reck'd she little of all that gay band,
But still cast her long-looking gaze o'er the land;
And smiled not, though often she turnèd and sigh'd,
Till a snowy-white courser afar she espied?

Sweet Mary, twin rose of the Asshèton line,
Was she who came forth like a Dian divine;
And often the knight and the damsel, of late,
Had met at the hunting, through love or through fate;
And now she bade welcome with maidenly pride—
The knight waved his hand and rode on by her side;
But ere the old woodlands of Bowlee were cross'd,
Both knight and fair maid to the hunters were lost.

For there, while the chase hurries on like the wind,
The twain of young lovers have tarried behind;
And leaving their steeds, the deep woodlands they pace,
His arm round the maid, and his looks on her face;
He whispers sweet words from his heart's inmost core,
He would love her through life and through death,—
 could he more?
And fondly, in tears, she emplighteth her vow,
"In life and in death I'll be faithful as thou!"

PART SECOND.

Now unto fair Alkrington tidings there came,
And soon was the knight made aware of the same,
That Mary, his loved one, was held in deep thrall,
Close bolted and barr'd, down at Middleton Hall;
And that her old father had sworn by his life,
His daughter should ne'er to Sir Ashton be wife;
And that one Sir Morden,* a knight from South-land,
Had come down to claim Lady Mary's fair hand.

Oh! woe unto true love, when kindred severe
Would stifle affection and chill its warm tear!
And woe unto true love, when trials come fast,
And friendship is found but a shadow at last!
And woe to the heart that is reft of its own,
And bidden to languish in sorrow alone!
But woe beyond weeping is that when we prove
That one we love dearly hath ceasèd to love!

Thus mournful the fate of the maid did appear;
Her sire, though he loved her, was stern and austere,
And friends who came round her when bright was her day,
Were silent, or doubtful, or kept quite away.
But Hope, like an angel, bright visions still drew,
And pictured her knight ever constant and true,
Till one came and told her he'd ta'en him a bride;—
Her young heart then wither'd, her tears were all dried.

How sweet is the music of wedding-day bells,
On sunny bright uplands, and down the green dells;
All gaily melodious it comes in the air,
As if undying pleasure were carolling there;
Like golden-wing'd seraphs all broken astray,
And playing on cymbals for bright holiday!
E'en such was the music one gay morning time,
Which the bells of St Leonards did merrily chime.

And why rang St Leonards that merry-mad tune?
And why was the church path with flowers bestrewn?
And who was that marble-pale beauty that moved
As nothing she hoped for, and nothing she loved—
Who gave her white hand, but 'twas clammy and cold?
Who sigh'd when she look'd on her ring of bright gold?
O Mary! lost Mary! where now is thy vow,
" In life and in death I'll be faithful as thou?"

---

\* This is a misnomer, as the monument of the last of the Asshetons in Middleton church testifies. The name should be Harbord.

## PART THIRD.

In a ruinous cottage, at Cambeshire barn,
An old wither'd crone sat unravelling yarn;
A few heapèd embers lay dusty and white;
A lamp, green and fetid, cast ominous light;
A cat strangely bark'd, as it hutch'd by the hob;
A broody hen crow'd from her perch on a cob;
The lamp it burn'd pale, and the lamp it burn'd blue,
And fearfully ghast was the light which it threw.

" And who cometh here ?" said the mumbling old crone,
" And why comes a gentleman riding alone?
And why doth he wander areawt\* such a night,
When the moon is gone down and the stars not alight;
When those are abroad would stab a lost child,
And the wind comes up muttering, fearful and wild,
And the hen 'gins to crow, and the dog 'gins to mew,
And my grave-fatted lamp glimmers dimly and blue?

"When the dog 'gins to mew, and the cat 'gins to bark,
And yon musty old skull snaps its teeth in the dark,
And the toad and the urchin crawl in from the moor,
And the frightful black adder creeps under the door,
And the hapless self-murder'd, that died in her sin,
Comes haunting the house with her dolorous din,
And stands in the nook like an image of clay,
With the sad look she wore when her life pass'd away."

A knocking was heard at the old hovel door,
And forth stepp'd a dark muffled man on the floor;
He threw back his mantle of many a fold,
And he cross'd the wan palm of the sibyl with gold.
" Now Sir Knight of Alkrington, what wouldst thou know,
That, seeking my home, thou entreatest me so?
The world-sweeping mower thy heart-wound must cure,
But she who lies mourning hath more to endure!

---

\* Areawt—out of doors—abroad.

" But warning I give thee, a sign from afar—
There's a cloud on thy sun, there's a spot on thy star.
Go, climb the wild mountain, or toil on the plain,
Or be outcast on land, or be wreck'd on the main;
Or seek the red battle, and dare the death-wound,
Or mine after treasure a mile under ground;
For, sleeping or waking, on ocean or strand,
Thy life is prolong'd, if thou hold thine own hand."

What further was said 'twixt the knight and the crone,
Was never repeated, and never was known;
But when he came back, to remount him again,
One, fearful and dark, held his stirrup and rein—
His horse, terror-shaking, stood cover'd with foam;
It ran with him miles ere he turn'd it towards home;
The gray morning broke, and the battle-cock crew,
Ere the lorn-hearted knight to his chamber withdrew.

### PART FOURTH.

And who hath not heard how the knight, from that day,
Was alter'd in look, and unwont in his way;
And how he sought wonders of every form,
And things of all lands, from a gem to a worm;
And how he divided his father's domain,
And sold many parts, to the purchasers' gain;
And how his poor neighbours with pity were sad,
And said, Good Sir Ashton, through love, was gone
  mad?

But strangest of all, on that woe-wedding night,
A black horse was stabled where erst stood the white;
The grooms, when they fed him, in terror quick fled,
His breath was hot smoke, and his eyes burning red;
He beat down a strong wall of mortar and crag;
He tore his oak stall, as a dog would a rag,
And no one durst put forth a hand near that steed,
Till a priest had read ave, and pater, and creed.

B

And then he came forth, the strange, beautiful thing,
With speed that could lead a wild eagle on wing;
And raven had never spread plume on the air,
Whose lustreful darkness with his might compare.
He bore the young Ashton—none else could him ride—
O'er flood and o'er fell, and o'er quarry-pit wide;
The housewife she bless'd her, and held fast her child,
And the men swore both horse and his rider were wild.

And then, when the knight to the hunting-field came,
He rode as he sought rather death than his game;
He hallooed through woods where he'd wander'd of yore,
But the lost Lady Mary he never saw more!
And no one durst ride in the track where he led,
So fearful his leaps, and so madly he sped;
And in his wild frenzy he gallop'd one day
Down the church-steps at Rochdale and up the same way.

This story (says Mr Bamford) is mainly founded on traditionary reminiscences, many of which are current amongst the old people of the district. Sir Assheton Lever, of Alkrington, is still represented in these old stories as the accepted lover (accepted by the lady) of Miss Assheton, eldest daughter, and (with her sister Eleanor) co-heiress of Sir Ralphe Assheton, who was lord of all the lands of Middleton, Thornham, Pilsworth, Unsworth, Radcliffe, Great and Little Lever, and Ainsworth. Sir Ashton Lever was the first knight of his name, and the last. He was of a line not as anciently titled as the Asshetons, and consequently, as is supposed, his attentions were not quite agreeable to the proud old baronet. Some stories impute his rejection to a personal difference betwixt the two families. However it was, the breaking off of the match has always been considered by the residents of the district as unfortunate to both the properties ; that of Middleton might certainly as well have been annexed to Hanover as to Gunton. Sir Ashton Lever, in after years, expended vast sums in forming and establishing the Leverian Museum. He was an excellent bowman, and a fearless rider ; and tradition has handed down stories of feats of horsemanship analogous to those recited in the ballad, accompanied with sage insinuations that no horse could have carried him save one of more than earthly breed or human training. That he performed the daring feat of riding at full gallop down the long and precipitous flight of steps leading from Rochdale churchyard into Packer Street, and up again, is still considered as doubtless as is the existence of the steps which remain there. He latterly sold many farms and plots of land, for sums to be paid yearly during his life ; and, soon after, died suddenly at the Bull's-head Inn in Manchester. Rumour said, at the time, that he died by his own hand. The lady was married to Harbord Harbord, Esq., nephew and heir of Sir William Morden, of Gunton, Norfolk, and afterwards the first Lord Suffield, who took, with her, the estates of Middleton and Thornham. After marriage, the lady seldom visited the hall of her fathers, and the ancient portion of it was levelled with the ground. It was one of the finest old relics of the sort in the county ; built of frame-work and plaster ; with pannels, carvings, and massy black beams, strong enough for a mill floor. The yard was entered through a low wicket, at a ponderous gate ; the interior was laid with small diamond-shaped flags ; a door on the left led into a large and lofty hall, hung round with matchlocks, steel caps, swords, targets, and hunting-weapons, intermixed with trophies of the battlefield and the chase. But all disappeared before the spirit of vandalism which commanded the annihilation of that most interesting relic of an ancient line. With respect to the other personages and accessories in the story, it may be mentioned that "the withered crone" was in being in the author's days. "Owd Mal o' Cambeshur" was a name of terror to the children, and of questionable import to their elders. The "ruinous cottage" at Cambeshire has fared better than the bride's chamber at the lordly hall. It has been improved, and is now inhabited by the family of a weaver. The place is at Cambeshire, on the top of Bowlee, in the township of Heaton. Sometimes it is called "Katty Green." "The old woodlands of Bowlee" have long since disappeared before the axe; and all the best timber of the two townships of Middleton and Thornham has shared the same fate: the country has, in fact, been pretty well swept out.

## A LEGEND OF THE HEART.

### By John Bolton Rogerson.

The lights have vanish'd one by one,
Till every taper's blaze hath gone;
The moonbeams through each casement creep,
And all seems hush'd in death-like sleep.

Young Imma lists with anxious ear,
But not a single sound can hear;
She leaves the chamber of her rest
And couch of snowy white unpress'd.

With silent footsteps steals the maid,
And starteth oft, as though afraid
The beatings of her heart are heard,
That flutters like a captive bird.

With cautious step she treads each stair,
Her light foot dwells a moment there;
Around a hurried glance is thrown,
And then again she glideth on.

Now she hath pass'd the winding stairs,
And with a quicker pace repairs
Along the wide and high-roof'd hall,
Till she hath gain'd the outer wall.

The pale moon shines on dark-green tree,
The low wind sighs its minstrelsy,
And, shaken from the shrub and flower,
The bright dew falls in silver shower.

She hurries on, the lovely one,
Around her form a mantle thrown;
Whilst pours the sweet-voiced nightingale
Upon her ear its mournful tale.

She passeth, as a star when driven
Along the cloudless face of heaven;
Her fair hair floating in the wind:
Tree, shrub, and flower are left behind.

A bounding tread is heard, a rush,
And to her face upsprings the blush;
To earth are cast her fawn-like eyes,
Whilst to her arms a dear one flies.

Yes! they had chosen that still hour,
When all was hush'd in hall and bower,
To meet—no witness to their love,
Save gleaming moon, that smiled above.

But who is he that meeteth there
That lady, graceful, proud, and fair?
Why doth she leave her father's hall,
And steal beyond the outer wall?

The youth is one of low estate,
The maiden's sire is rich and great;
But what cares love for high degree?
He laughs at wealth and ancestry.

Ever are secret raptures sweet—
The youth is at the lady's feet;
He poureth forth impassion'd sighs,
And readeth answers in her eyes.

Oh! would that you had never met,
For watchful spies are round you set;
The aged sire, in furious mood,
Is bent upon a deed of blood.

There comes a swift and wingèd dart,
Which cleaves its way through beating heart,
And he who lately blest her charms
Lies dead within the lady's arms!

And shall I tell the maiden's fate?
She lived on long, though desolate;
Better had she been with the dead,
For reason's guiding-star had fled.

Though by her kindred guarded well,
When shades of night around her fell,
She ever left her father's hall,
And wander'd round the outer wall.

It is a legend of old date,
Which ancient gossips oft narrate,
And some who tell the mournful tale,
Say they have heard the lady's wail.

They tell that still her form is seen,
Gliding the moon's white rays between,
That she may mourn the hapless fate
Of him who died through love and hate.

## BALLAD.

### By Charles Swain.

Why leave you thus your father's hall,
    And hie to the gate so oft?
'Tis only to watch the moonlight fall
    O'er the waves that sleep so soft.
And why do you seek one small blue flower
    Through every sylvan spot?
Oh, 'tis but a gem for a maiden's bower,
    A little " forget-me-not ! "

Why wear you that wreath so dim and dry,
    With its leaves all pined and dead?
The maid look'd up with a tearful eye,
    But never a word she said.
And why for every word you speak
    Have you twenty sighs of late?
The maiden hath hied, with a blushing cheek,
    Again to the moonlit gate.

Hark!  Is it a sound, indeed, that rings?
    A hoof o'er the wild road press'd?
Oh, is it her own true knight that springs
    And folds her to his breast?
And is it that *wreath* so dark and dry
    That meets her knight's fond kiss?
Again was a tear in the maiden's eye,
    But oh! 'twas a tear of bliss!

## THE MANDRAKE.

### By William Harrison Ainsworth.

The mandrake grows 'neath the gallows tree,
And rank and green are its leaves to see;
Green and rank as the grass that waves
Over the unctuous earth of graves,
And though all around it be bleak and bare,
Freely the mandrake flourisheth there.
    Maranatha—Anathema!
   Dread is the curse of Mandragora!
     Euthanasy!

At the foot of the gibbet the mandrake springs,
Just where the creaking carcase swings;
Some have thought it engenderèd
From the fat that drops from the bones of the dead;
Some have thought it a human thing;
But this is a vain imagining.
    Maranatha—Anathema!
   Dread is the curse of Mandragora!
     Euthanasy!

A charnel leaf doth the mandrake wear,
A charnel fruit doth the mandrake bear;
Yet none like the mandrake hath such great power,
Such virtues reside not in herb or flower;
Aconite, hemlock, or moonshade, I ween,
None hath a poison so subtle and keen.
    Maranatha—Anathema!
   Dread is the curse of Mandragora!
     Euthanasy!

And whether the mandrake be create
Flesh with the flower incorporate,

---

Editors Note: Mandrake is a plant associated with evil, and said to be used in spells and witchcraft.

I know not; yet if from the earth 'tis rent,
Shrieks and groans from the root are sent;
Shrieks and groans, and a sweat like gore,
Oozes and drops from the clammy core.
    Maranatha—Anathema!
   Dread is the curse of Mandragora!
    Euthanasy!

Whoso gathereth the mandrake shall surely die!
Blood for blood is his destiny.
Some who have pluck'd it have died with groans,
Like to the mandrake's expiring moans;
Some have died raving, and some beside,
With penitent prayers—but *all* have died.
    Jesu! save us, by night and by day!
   From the terrible death of Mandragora!
    Euthanasy!

---

This song was written to accompany the book 'Lancashire Witches'

## THE HUNTER'S SONG.

(A BALLAD SUPPOSED TO HAVE BEEN WRITTEN ABOUT THE BEGINNING OF THE EIGHTEENTH CENTURY.)

By the late Rev. Richard Parkinson, D.D.

WITH staff in hand, the hunter stood
   On Radholme's dewy lawn;
And still he watch'd in anxious mood,
   The first faint streaks of dawn.
Faintly on Pendle's height they play'd,
   The thrush began to sing,
The doe forsook the hazel shade,
   The heron left his spring.

He turn'd him east—the Ribble there
   In waves of silver roll'd,
While every cloud that sail'd in air
   Just wore a tinge of gold.
There Waddow's meads, so bright and green,
   Had caught the early ray,
And there, through shadow dimly seen,
   Rose Clid'row's Castle gray.

He turn'd him west, and hill o'er hill,
   Fair Bowland Knotts were seen,
Emerging from the mists that fill
   The winding vales between.
The thorns that crown'd each verdant crest,
   Look'd greener to the eye,
While vistas, opening to the west,
   Display'd a crimson sky.

But most he turn'd where, 'neath his feet,
   The Hodder murmur'd by,
And yon low cot, so trim and neat,
   Still fix'd the hunter's eye.
He gazed, as lovers wont to gaze,
   Then gaily thus he sang,—
From Browsholme Heights to Batter Heys
   The mountain echoes rang.

"Fair is my love, as mountain snow,
    All other snows excelling,
And gentle as the timid roe
    That bounds around her dwelling;
With other maids I oft have roved,
    And maids of high degree,
But none like her have look'd and loved—
    My Anna still for me!

" When at her door she sits to sing
    Some simple strain of mine,
The lark will poise him on the wing
    To catch the notes divine;
And when she speeds her love to meet
    Across the broomy lee;
The dew that sparkles round her feet
    Is not so bright as she.

"Around the Fairy Oak* I've seen
    The gentle fairies dancing,
And, mounted light, in robes of green,
    O'er Radholme gaily prancing;
On moonlit eve I've seen them play
    Around their crystal well,†
But lovelier far than elf or fay
    Is Anna of the dell!

" And still, though poor and lowly born,
    To me she's kind and true;
She flies the Bowman's‡ tassell'd horn,
    She shuns the bold Buccleugh.§
Old Rose‖ may rule by word and sigh,
    By magic art and spell;
But what are all her charms to thine,
    Sweet Anna of the dell?"

---

\* Now corruptly called Fairoak.    † The White Well.
‡ Parker, of Browsholme.    § Chief Forester.
‖ A noted witch of the time.

## A BALLAD.

#### By John Bolton Rogerson.

"Cast the gay robes from off thy form,
    And cease thine hair to braid;
Thy love to thee will come no more,
    He wooes another maid;
And broken are the many vows
    That he hath pledged to thee—
He wooes another maid, and this
    His bridal morn will be!"


"False unto me! Oh, say not so;
    For if thy tale be true,
And he I love be lost to me,
    I shall not live to rue;
If he do take another mate
    Before the holy shrine;
Another ne'er shall have my heart,—
    Death will be mate of mine!"


She cast the gay robes from her form,
    And donn'd a snow-white gown:
She loosen'd from her locks the braid,
    And let them droop adown;
She flung around her lovely head
    The thin shroud of her veil,
To hide her fast-descending tears,
    And cheek as moon-ray pale.

With feeble, yet with hurried steps,
    Unto the church she hied,
And there she saw the false of heart
    Receive another bride!
The bridal pageant swept along
    Till all the train had fled—
Why stay'd the lone, deserted one?
    She slumber'd with the dead!

## KING FROST.

### By Charles Swain.

King Frost gallop'd hard from his Palace of Snow,
To the hills whence the floods dash'd in thunders below!
But he breathed on the waters that swoon'd at his will,
And their clamour was o'er, for the torrents stood still!
" Ho! ho!" thought the king, as he gallop'd along,
" I have stopp'd those mad torrents a while in their song."

With pennons high streaming, in gladness and pride,
A fair vessel moved o'er the billowy tide;
But, whilst bold hearts were deeming their perils all past,
King Frost struck the billows, and fetter'd them fast!
" Ho! ho!" cried the monarch, "their homes may long wait,
Ere aught, my fine vessel, be heard of your fate!"

Through the forest rode he, and the skeleton trees
Groan'd, wither'd and wild, 'gainst the desolate breeze;
And shook their hoar locks, as the Frost King flew by,
Whilst the hail rattled round, like a volley from high!
" Ho! ho!" shouted he, " my old Sylvans, ye're bare;
But my minister Snow shall find robes for your wear!"

By the convent sped he—by the lone, ruin'd fane,
Where the castle frown'd wild o'er its rocky domain;
And the warder grew pallid, and shook as in fear,
As the monarch swept by, with his icicle spear!
Whilst his herald, the Blast, breathed defiance below,
And hurrah'd for King Frost and his Palace of Snow!

## CLAYTON HALL.

### By Elijah Ridings.

CLAYTON HALL is an old moated edifice, in the township of Droylsden, once the residence of the baronial Byrons, and afterwards a favourite home of Humphrey Chetham. It is a quaint, half-timbered house, with bell-turret and bell, and in the olden time was duly provided, like most old halls of Lancashire, with its ghost, which was so regular in its visitations that it gave rise to the proverbial saying, "Here aw come agen, loike Clayton Ho Boggart."

    The bell doth call, in Clayton Hall,
        The labourer from his bed ;
    The day hath dawn'd, blithe Hodge hath yawn'd
        And from his cot hath sped ;
    With pick and spade on shoulder laid,
        With rustic smockfrock gray,
    With hardy face and homely grace,
        To work he hies away.

    Hath sentinel of old Cromwell
        E'er watch'd thine ancient hall ?
    Thine olden bower hath seen the hour
        Of royal Charles's fall ;
    O'er thy threshhold hath warrior bold
        E'er pass'd with manly tread ?
    Have drums e'er beat around thy seat,
        Or martial banners spread ?

Let fancy float around thy moat,
    Which since his day hath been;
Thy looks are gray, to time a prey,
    A melancholy scene;
Thy ruin'd tower, thy lonely bower,
    To thoughtful minds recall
The civil wars, rebellion's jars,
    O venerable Hall!

Those days are gone, but their dread tone
    Reviveth at my call,
And doth mingle in the dingle
    That blooms around the Hall,
With the loud songs of feather'd throngs,
    Whose varied wonders fall
In all their powers o'er my lone hours,
    O ancient Clayton Hall!

With grateful grace may I retrace
    The merchant prince,* whose name
And pious, charitable face,
    Are dedicate to fame;
While there is either book or stone
    To tell that he hath been,
His venerable name alone
    Shall consecrate this scene.

---

\* Humphrey Chetham, Esq., founder of the Hospital, School, and Library in Manchester which bear his name. He resided at Clayton Hall, about three miles east of Manchester, and closed his useful life there in 1653.

## THE WANDERER.

### By Charles Swain.

Three dreary years in peril tost,
 Three years upon a polar sea,
Ice-wreck'd, and half his comrades lost,
 Once more his native land treads he.

While westward from the sandy height,
 He views where, far, his cottage lies,
A father's transport fills his sight,
 A husband's joy o'erflows his eyes.

He speeds by each remember'd way,
 Each turning brings him still more near;
He sees his first-born child at play,
 And calls, but cannot make him hear.

Fast as he speeds, his child appears
 Still distant as it was before;
At length, with bursting, grateful tears,
 He sees his young wife at the door.

She takes the sweet child by the hand,
 She kisses him with loving joy;
The gazer deems in all the land
 There's no such other wife or boy.

She lifts him fondly to her cheek,
 Then leaves the narrow wicket gate;
The Wanderer thinks he will not speak,
 But gaze and wait—if love can wait.

But from that gate, to open view,
   Come never more those feet so light ;
There grew no covert, that he knew,
   Whose leaves might hide them from his sight.

A sudden terror fills his veins,
   And chills the rapture in his eyes ;
With eager spring the gate he gains,
   And calls, but not a voice replies.

The door, it does not stand ajar,
   The casement, too, is closed and dark ;
Across the path is thrown a bar,
   And all wears Desolation's mark.

He shrieks in fear each name so dear—
   The garden plot is waste and wild ;
O God ! why doth his wife not hear ?
   O Love ! why cometh not his child ?


He strains to catch the slightest trace
   Of form or raiment ; nought is seen,
As with a wild and spectral face,
   The gray boughs groan and intervene.

The leaves bend trembling to their root,
   The frail grass mutters to the flower ;
With ghost-like wing the long rays shoot,
   While tolls the bell the vesper hour.

He turns, bewilder'd at the sound—
   Again his wife, his child, appear ;
They move across the churchyard ground,
   And beckon the pale Wanderer near.

A few more steps and he may hold
   The twain within his trembling arms ;
Why seems his sinking heart so cold ?
   What chokes him with those dread alarms ?

Pale, in the dreary moonlight, gleams
   Each mound and monumental stone ;
He stands distraught, as one that dreams—
   Was he again alone—alone ?

Alone—they've pass'd, yet nothing stirr'd!
　　He thought that through the spectral air
There rose one low, one little word,
　　Faint echo of some infant prayer.

He thought that name which erst had moved
　　His pulses with a parent's joy,
Came softly, as in hours beloved,
　　When on his glad knee sat his boy.

Yet all had fled; and on the stone,
　　Beneath his feet, two lines were read,
Sad lines, that to the eyes once shown,
　　Do break the heart that's better dead.

He press'd his hot lips to each name,
　　He kiss'd each letter o'er and o'er;
They scorch'd his sight, as if with flame,
　　They sear'd his worn heart to the core.

" For this," he cried, " for this was won
　　My way through tempests—this to bear;
Still, still, O God! Thy will be done!
　　Yet one—not one!—not one to spare!"

Morn stepp'd from out the mists of heaven,
　　And coldly lit each hallow'd spot;
Another morn to him was given,
　　Another world where death was not!

## THE BILLMEN OF BOWLAND.

FROM "NED OF THE FELL"—A LANCASHIRE ROMANCE.

AGAINST tenfold his numbers on Agincourt's plain,
The gallant King Henry the fight must maintain ;
No knight like young Harry had England e'er known,
A pillar of fire to his army he shone ;
His troops throng'd around him, they darken'd the field,
And the Billmen of Bowland swore never to yield.

His red-hair'd Northumbrian vassals were there,
And Durham and Cumberland brandish'd the spear ;
The Londoners, too, in their trimmest array,
And the yeomen of Kent, who delight in a fray ;
But from father to son old tradition hath told
That the Billmen of Bowland were best of the bold.

There Yorkshire and Durham did courage evince,
And the men of old Monmouth defended their prince ;
The archers of Nottingham bent the long bow,
And their arrows were dyed in the blood of the foe ;
But with axes uplifted, that gleam'd in the light,
The Billmen of Bowland were first in the fight.

From the banks of Sabrina they rush'd to the plain,
And Devon's proud heroes were found midst the slain ;
And the children of Cornwall, as rude as their soil,
Exultingly shared in the glory and spoil ;
But the Billmen of Bowland, old Lancashire's pride,
Stood firm as the hills, and the foemen defied.

Resistance was vain ; neither falchion nor mail,
Nor helmet, nor shield-cover'd arm could avail ;
When our foresters struck, death follow'd each wound,
The steed and his rider alike bit the ground.
There was glory for England on Agincourt's day,
But the Billmen of Bowland the palm bore away.

## BLACK BESS.

### By William Harrison Ainsworth.

Let the lover his mistress's beauty rehearse,
And laud her attractions in languishing verse;
Be it mine in rude strains, but with *truth* to express
The love that I bear to my bonny Black Bess.

From the West was her dam, from the East was her sire,
From the one came her swiftness, the other her fire;
No peer of the realm better blood can possess,
Than flows in the veins of my bonny Black Bess.

Look! look! how that eyeball glows bright as a brand!
That neck proudly arches, those nostrils expand!
Mark that wide-flowing mane! of which each silky tress
Might adorn prouder beauties — though none like Black Bess.

Mark that skin sleek as velvet, and dusky as night,
With its jet undisfigured by one lock of white;
That throat branch'd with veins, prompt to charge or caress;
Now is she not beautiful? bonny Black Bess!

Over highway and byway, in rough and smooth weather,
Some thousands of miles have we journey'd together;
Our couch the same straw, and our meal the same mess,
No couple more constant than I and Black Bess!

By moonlight, in darkness, by night, or by day,
Her headlong career there is nothing to stay ;
She cares not for distance, she knows not distress :
Can you show me a courser to match with Black Bess?

Once it happen'd in Cheshire, near Dunham, I popp'd
On a horseman alone, whom I suddenly stopp'd ;
That I lighten'd his pockets you 'll readily guess—
Quick work makes Dick Turpin when mounted on
    Bess.

Now it seems the man knew me ; "Dick Turpin," said
    he
"You shall swing for this job, as you live, d'ye see."
I laugh'd at his threats and his vows of redress,
I was sure of an alibi then with Black Bess.

The road was a hollow, a sunken ravine,*
Overshadow'd completely by wood like a screen ;
I clamber'd the bank, and I needs must confess,
That one touch of the spur grazed the side of Black
    Bess.

Brake, brook, meadow, and plough'd field, Bess fleetly
    bestrode,
As the crow wings her flight, we selected our road ;
We arrived at Hough Green in five minutes, or less—
My neck it was saved by the speed of Black Bess.

---

  * The exact spot where Turpin committed this robbery, which has often been pointed out to me, (writes Mr Harrison Ainsworth,) lies in what is now a woody hollow, though once the old road from Altrincham to Knutsford, skirting Dunham Park, and descending the hill that brings you to the bridge crossing the river Bollin. With some difficulty I penetrated this ravine. It is just the place for an adventure of the kind. A small brook wells through it, and the steep banks are overhung with timber, and were, when I last visited the place, in April 1834, a perfect nest of primroses and wild-flowers. Hough (pronounced *Hoo*) Green lies about three miles across the country—the way Turpin rode. The old Bowling-green used to be one of the pleasantest inns in Cheshire.

Stepping carelessly forward, I lounge on the green,
Taking excellent care that by all I am seen;
Some remarks on Time's flight to the squires I address;
But I say not a word of the flight of Black Bess.

I mention the hour—it was just about four—
Play a rubber at bowls—think the danger is o'er;
When athwart my next game, like a checkmate at chess,
Comes the horseman in search of the rider of Bess.

What matter details? Off with triumph I came;
He swears to the hour, and the squires swear the same;
I had robb'd him at *four!*—while at four *they* profess,
I was quietly bowling—all thanks to Black Bess!

Then one halloo, boys, one loud cheering halloo!
To the swiftest of coursers, the gallant, the true!
For the sportsman unborn shall the memory bless
Of the horse of the highwayman—bonny Black Bess!

## GYPSY BALLAD.

### By Charles Swain.

What care we for earth's renown !
  We to greenwood pleasures born :
Tinsel makes an easier crown
  Than the proudest kings have worn.
Though our royal sword of state
  Be a feeble willow wand ;
Courtiers have been glad to wait
  For the pretty Gypsy's hand !
    Underneath the old oak tree,
      Soon as sets the summer day,
    Gypsy lads and lasses we,
      Dance and sing the night away.

Many bind their hours with care,
  Labour through the anxious day,
Just to gain enough to bear
  Corpse and coffin to the clay !
Though but little we may claim,
  Still that little we enjoy ;
Wealth is often but a name ;
  Title but a gilded toy !
    Underneath the old oak tree, &c.

## OLD GRINDROD'S GHOST.

AT the end of Cross Lane, formerly called Pendleton Moor, a woolcomber in Salford, named John Grindrod (or Grindret) was gibbeted in March 1759, (Baines dates the deed in 1753,) for poisoning his wife and two children with brimstone and treacle in the preceding September. Connected with this man there is a ghostly legend, telling of a boastful traveller, who lost a foolish wager on a tempestuous night; and of an eccentric skeleton that was in the habit of taking midnight walks, for the purpose of dispelling the wetness and weariness occasioned by long suspension.


Old Grindrod was hang'd on a gibbet high,
    On a spot where the dark deed was done;
'Twas a desolate place, on the edge of a moor,
    A place for the timid to shun.

Chains round his middle, and chains round his neck,
    And chains round his ankles were hung;
And there in all weathers, in sunshine and rain,
    Old Grindrod the murderer swung.

Old Grindrod had long been the banquet of crows,
    Who flock'd on his carcase to batten;
And the unctuous morsels that fell from their feast,
    Served the rank weeds beneath him to fatten.

All that's now left of him is a skeleton grim,
    The stoutest to strike with dismay;
So ghastly the sight, that no urchin, at night,
    Who can help it, will pass by that way.

All such as had dared, had sadly been scared,
   And soon 'twas the general talk,
That the wretch in his chains, each night took the pains,
   To come down from the gibbet—*and walk!*

The story was told to a traveller bold,
   At an inn near the moor, by the host;
He appeals to each guest, and its truth they attest,
   But the traveller laughs at the ghost.

" Now to show you," quoth he, " how afraid I must be,
   A rump and a dozen I'll lay,
That before it strikes one, I will go forth alone,
   Old Grindrod a visit to pay.

" To the gibbet I'll go, and this I will do,
   As sure as I stand in my shoes;
Some address I'll devise, and if Grinny replies,
   My wager of course I shall lose."

" Accepted the bet; but the night it is wet,"
   Quoth the host. " Never mind," says the guest;
" From darkness and rain the adventure will gain
   To my mind an additional zest."

Now midnight had toll'd, and the traveller bold
   Set out from the inn all alone;
'Twas a night black as ink, and our friend 'gan to think
   That uncommonly cold it had grown.

But of nothing afraid, and by nothing delay'd,
   Plunging onward through bog and through wood,
Wind and rain in his face, he ne'er slacken'd his pace,
   Till under the gibbet he stood.

Though dark as could be, yet he thought he could see
   The skeleton hanging on high;
The gibbet it creaked, and the rusty chains squeaked,
   And a screech-owl flew solemnly by.

The heavy rain patter'd, the hollow bones clatter'd,
   The traveller's teeth chatter'd—with cold—not with fright;
The wind it blew lustily, piercingly, gustily;
   Certainly not an agreeable night!

"Ho! Grindrod, old fellow!" thus loudly did bellow
　　The traveller mellow,—"How are you, my blade?"
"I'm cold and I'm dreary; I'm wet and I'm weary;
　　But soon I'll be near ye!" the skeleton said.


The grisly bones rattled, and with the chains battled;
　　The gibbet appallingly shook;
On the ground something stirr'd, but no more the man heard—
　　To his heels on the instant he took.

## THE KEEPER'S SON.

### By R. R. Bealey.

No braver lad e'er walk'd the wood,
    No fairer lad could be,
Than Johnny Brown, the Keeper's son,
    Who lived at Walker Lea.
Shouldering gun he forth would go,
    Nor tire the longest day,
With faithful "Don" close up "to heel,"
    His work was always play.


They'd wander through the wooded glen,
    Or climb the mountain high,
They'd cross the stubble fields, and walk
    As softly as a sigh;
And if a bird should chance to rise,
    Or rabbit dare to run,
'Twould surely fall beneath the shot
    Of Johnny's fatal gun.


One morn with faithful "Don" he went,
    ('Twas in October chill,)
To have a little early sport
    Beneath the western hill;
When, firing at a brace of birds,
    And thinking all was well,
The gun it burst, and on the ground
    The bleeding sportsman fell.

All senseless on the ground he lay,
    But " Don" was by his side,
And when he saw his master bleed,
    The faithful dog, he cried ;
He lick'd the wounds with tender care,
    Then by his side he lay,
To keep his master's body warm
    On that October day.


'Twas very sad, for on that night,
    At dusk, John did agree
To meet the miller's daughter Jane
    Beneath the chestnut tree.
She went and waited, but, alas !
    She waited all in vain ;
And tears were falling down her cheeks,
    As home she walk'd again.

The wound was fatal, and poor John,
    He never breathèd more ;
And Jane, she could not love again,
    But widow's weeds she wore.
The dog and she together live,
    And day by day they go
To see the spot where Johnny Brown,
    The Keeper's son, lies low !

## THE BALLAD OF JAMES AND JANE.*

\* James I. of Scotland—the youthful poet of "The King's Quhair"—was long a prisoner in Windsor Castle. He was deeply enamoured of the Lady Jane Beaufort, a daughter of the Earl of Somerset, who afterwards became his queen. This king was assassinated at Perth in 1437.

BY HENRY KIRK.

SAD was Scotland's king!
   He saw no hope in the morrow;
Not a tone from his harp could he bring
   That spoke not language of sorrow.

He gazed from his latticed room;
   Nought in the scene before him
Had power to lighten the gloom
   His dreary fate threw o'er him.

The moon sinking westerly,
   The stars from the zenith beaming,
Silver'd each turret and tree,
   But brighten'd not his dreaming.

Cut off in his youth for life,
   Bright spirit of chivalry! Never
In the tourney's mimic strife
   To contend for a lady's favour.

The thought of the state, bereft him;
   He fear'd for his people's woe;
He wept the chance that had left him
   The thrall of a jealous foe.*

---

\* Henry IV. of England.

Full of high ambition,
   In prison to live and die!
Despair foreshadow'd perdition
   From his deep lustreless eye.

As calm, after tempest howling,
   To mariners out at sea,
As sunshine, after the scowling
   Of clouds on a summer lea,—

Came a change o'er the minstrel king;
   No more did he pine and languish,
Or from his wild harp wring
   Accents of doleful anguish.

Now full of a tender pleasure,
   His happy harp and tongue;
For love had blest his measure
   With the richest charm of song.

Often his sweet lay pouring
   Through the twilight's stilly haze,
Men thought to be angels adoring
   Their God in anthems of praise.

And ever his pleasant fancies
   Dwelt on his promised queen,
With blue eyes and passionate glances,
   And hair of a golden sheen.

In visions of night and day,
   A glorious future gathers,
Where he wields with princely sway
   The sceptred might of his fathers.

And now Love's gentle hand
   Hath freed the fetters that bound him;
He is king in his own wild land,
   With its mountains and heather around him.

With love ever true and tender,
  Never was monarch so blest;
It was sweet from state's thorny splendour
  To repose on his fond queen's breast.

When he fell from the cruel wounds
  Of Graham, traitor disloyal!
In the convent's holy bounds,
  By Perth's proud city royal,—

Thrice did the dagger pierce her;
  Faster the fond queen clung
To shield her lover, fiercer
  Than lioness shields her young.

Ever while love and song
  The sons of Scotland cherish,
James shall be first among
  The names that may not perish!

Ever, while Windsor s towers
  A pilgrim's steps detain,
He shall seek the moated bowers
  Of the stately and gentle Jane!

## DERWENTWATER'S FATE:

#### A BALLAD.

IN the *Gentleman's Magazine* for June 1825, (page 489,) is a letter from a correspondent, signing G. H., accompanied by what he calls "An old song on the death of Radcliffe, Earl of Derwentwater, who was beheaded as a traitor on Tower Hill, February 24, 1716. It was one of the most popular in its day in the north of England, for a long period after the event which it records had taken place. I took it down (says this correspondent) from the dictation of an old person, who had learned it from her father. In its oral descent from generation to generation, it had got a little corrupted. But a poetical friend of mine has assisted me in restoring it to something like poetical propriety. My dictator could not go further than the seventeenth verse, and supposed it ended there; but it seemed defective. The last four verses are now added to give a finish. There is a pathetic simplicity in the song at once affecting and interesting, and which renders it, I think, deserving of preservation."

> King George he did a letter write,
>   And seal'd it up with gold,
> And sent it to Lord Derwentwater
>   To read it, if he could.
>
> He sent his letter by no post,
>   He sent it by no page;
> But sent it by a gallant knight,
>   As e'er did combat wage.
>
> The first line that my lord look'd on,
>   Struck him with strong surprise;
> The second, more alarming still,
>   Made tears fall from his eyes.

He callèd up his stable-groom,
   Saying, "Saddle me well my steed;
For I must up to London go,—
   Of me there seems great need."

His lady, hearing what he said,
   As she in childbed lay,
Cried, " My dear lord, pray make your will,
   Before you go away."

" I'll leave to thee, my eldest son,
   My houses and my land;
I'll leave to thee, my younger son,
   Ten thousand pounds in hand.

" I'll leave to thee, my lady gay,
   My lawful married wife,
A third part of my whole estate,
   To keep thee a lady's life."

He knelt him down by her bedside,
   And kiss'd her lips so sweet;
The words that pass'd, alas! presaged
   They never more should meet!

Again he call'd his stable-groom,
   Saying, " Bring me out my steed,
For I must up to London go,
   With instant haste and speed."

He took the reins into his hand,
   Which shook with fear and dread;
The rings from off his fingers dropp'd;
   His nose gush'd out and bled

He had but ridden miles two or three,
   When, stumbling, fell his steed;
" Ill omens these," Derwentwater said,
   " That I for James must bleed."

As he rode up Westminster Street,
   In sight of the White Hall,
The lords and ladies of London town
   A traitor they did him call.

"A traitor!" Lord Derwentwater said,
  "A traitor! How can I be,
Unless for keeping five hundred men,
  Fighting for King Jemmy?"

Then started forth a grave old man,
  With a broad-mouth'd axe in hand,
"Thy head, thy head, Lord Derwentwater,
  Thy head's at my command."

"My head, my head, thou grave old man,
  My head I will give thee;
Here's a coat of velvet on my back
  Will surely pay thy fee;

"But give me leave," Derwentwater said,
  "To speak words two or three;
Ye lords and ladies of London town,
  Be kind to my lady.

"Here's a purse of fifty sterling pounds,
  Pray give it to the poor;
Here's one of forty-five beside,
  You may dole from door to door."

He laid his head upon the block;
  The axe was sharp and strong;
The stroke that cut his sufferings short,
  His memory cherish'd long.

Thus fell proud Derwent's ancient lord,
  Dread victim to the laws;
His lands fell forfeit to the crown,
  Lost in the Stuarts' cause.

His weeping widow's drooping heart
  With sorrow burst in twain;
His orphan children, outcast, spurn'd,
  Deep felt th' attainted stain.

The Derwent's far-famed lake alone
  Its noble name retains;
And of the title, thence extinct,
  Sole monument remains.

## II.

## Love Songs and Praises of the Fair.

### LOVE'S EVIL CHOICE. *

* Mrs Habergham's husband was driven out of Habergham Hall for debt. She soothed herself writing stanzas. The following is copied from a broadside of about 1696. She was buried at Padiham in 1703.

I sow'd the seeds of love, it was all in the spring,
In April, May, and June likewise, when small birds they do sing;
My garden's well planted with flowers everywhere,
Yet I had not liberty to choose for myself the flower I loved so dear.

My gardener he stood by, I ask'd him to choose for me:
He chose me the violet, the lily, and pink, but these I refused all three:
The violet I forsook, because it fades so soon;
The lily and pink I did o'erlook, and I vow'd I'd stay till June.

In June there's a red rose-bud, and that's the flower for me!
But oft have I pluck'd at the red rose-bud, till I gain'd the willow-tree;

The willow-tree will twist, and the willow-tree will twine,
Oh! I wish I was in the dear youth's arms that once had this heart of mine.

My gardener he stood by, he told me to take great care,
For in the middle of a red rose-bud there grows a sharp thorn there;
I told him I'd take no care till I did feel the smart,
And often I pluck'd at the red rose-bud till I pierced it to the heart.

I'll make me a posy of hyssop,—no other I can touch,
That all the world may plainly see I love one flower too much;
My garden is run wild!—where shall I plant anew?
For my bed, that once was cover'd with thyme, is all overrun with rue.

Dr Whittaker gives a traditional version of part of this song, which, as far as it goes, is superior to the broadside copy:—

The gardener standing by, proffer'd to choose for me
The pink, the primrose, and the rose; but I refused the three;
The primrose I forsook, because it came too soon;
The violet I overlook'd, and vow'd to wait till June.

In June the red rose sprung, but was no flower for me;
I pluck'd it up, lo! by the stalk, and planted the willow-tree.
The willow I now must wear, with sorrows twined among,
That all the world may know I falsehood loved too long.

## THE SPRIG OF THYME.

(FROM A BROADSIDE IN THE GREAVES COLLECTION.)

You virgins far and near,
    That are just in your prime,
I'd have you keep your gardens clear,
    Let no one steal your thyme.

Once I had a sprig of thyme,
    And it flourish'd night and day,
Until there came a false young man,
    And he stole my thyme away.

But now my thyme's all gone,
    No more I can it see;
The man who stole my thyme away,
    He did prove false to me.

Since now my thyme's all gone,
    And I can plant no new,
In the very place where grew my thyme,
    It's overrun with rue.

Rue, rue, runs over all;
    But so it shall not seem,
For I'll plant again in the same place,
    And call it the willow green.

Willow, willow, I must wear,
    Willow, willow, is my doom,
Since my false love's forsaken me,
    And left me here to moan.

A gardener standing by,
    Three flowers he offer'd me,
The lily, pink, and red rose-bud,
    But I refused all three.

The pink it is a flower that's sweet,
    So is the rose in June;
The lily is the virgin flower,
    Alas! oft cropp'd too soon.

## COLIN AND PHEBE.

#### A PASTORAL.

#### By John Byrom, M.A., F.R.S.

This pastoral song was written while its author was a student at Trinity College, Cambridge. It was first printed in 1714 as No. 603 of the *Spectator*. The lady in whose praise it was written was Joanna, the youngest daughter of the celebrated Dr Bentley, Master of Trinity College. She was married to Dr Dennison Cumberland, Bishop of Clonfert, Ireland, and was mother of Richard Cumberland the dramatist. John Byrom was born at Manchester in 1691, and died September 28, 1763.

My time, O ye Muses, was happily spent,
When Phebe went with me wherever I went;
Ten thousand sweet pleasures I felt in my breast;
Sure never fond shepherd like Colin was blest!
But now she has gone and has left me behind,
What a marvellous change on a sudden I find!
When things seem'd as fine as could possibly be,
I thought 'twas the spring; but alas! it was she.

With such a companion to tend a few sheep,
To rise up and play, or to lie down and sleep,
So good-humour'd made me, so cheerful and gay,
My heart was as light as a feather all day.
But now I so cross and so peevish am grown,
So strangely uneasy as never was known.
My fair one is gone, and my joys are all drown'd;
And my heart, I am sure, weighs more than a pound.

The fountain that wont to run sweetly along,
And dance to soft murmurs the pebbles among,
Thou know'st, little Cupid, if Phebe was there,
'Twas pleasure to look at, 'twas music to hear.
But now she is absent, I walk by its side,
And still as it murmurs do nothing but chide;
" Must you be so cheerful, while I go in pain?
Peace there with your bubbling, and hear me com-
    plain."

When round me my lambkins would oftentimes play,
And Phebe and I were as joyful as they,
How pleasant their sporting, how happy the time
When spring, love, and beauty were all in their prime!
But now in their frolics, when by me they pass,
I fling at their fleeces a handful of grass;
" Be still!" then I cry, "for it makes me quite mad
To see you so merry while I am so sad."

My dog I was ever well pleased to see
Come wagging his tail to my fair one and me;
Phebe likewise was pleased, and to my dog said,
" Come hither, poor fellow!" and patted his head.
But now when he's fawning, I, with a sour look,
Cry " Sirrah!" and give him a blow with my crook.
And I'll give him another; for why should not Tray
Be as dull as his master when Phebe's away.

When walking with Phebe what sights have I seen!
How fair were the flowers, how fresh was the green!
What a lovely appearance the trees and the shade,
The corn-fields, the hedges, and everything made!
But now she has left me, they all are in tears,
Not one of them half so delightful appears;
'Twas nought but the magic, I find, of her eyes
That made all those beautiful prospects arise.

Sweet music attended us all the wood through,
The lark, linnet, throstle, and nightingale too;
Winds over us whisper'd, flocks by us did bleat,
And " chirp" went the grasshopper under our feet.

Now, since she is absent, though still they sing on,
The woods are but lonely, the melody's gone;
Her voice in the concert, as now I have found,
Gave everything else its agreeable sound.

Rose, what is become of thy delicate hue?
And where is the violet's beautiful blue?
Does aught of its sweetness the blossom beguile?
That meadow, those daisies, why do they not smile?
Ah! rivals, I see what it was, that you drest
And made yourselves fine for—a place in her breast;
You put on your colours to please her fine eye,
To be pluck'd by her hand, on her bosom to die.

How shortly time creeps! Till my Phebe return,
Amid the soft zephyr's cool breezes I burn!
Methinks if I knew whereabout he would tread,
I could breathe on his wings, it would melt down the lead.
Fly swifter, ye minutes, bring hither my dear,
And for it rest longer when she shall be here.
Ah! Colin, old Time is too full of delay,
Nor will budge one foot faster for all thou canst say.

Will no pitying power, that hears me complain,
Or cure my disquiet, or soften my pain?
To be cured thou must, Colin, thy passion remove;
Yet what swain is so silly to live without love?
No, deity, bid the dear nymph to return;
For ne'er was poor shepherd so sadly forlorn.
Ah! what shall I do? I shall die with despair!
Take heed all ye swains how ye part with your fair!

## SONGS.

### By William Rowlinson of Manchester.

This rhymester was for some time a clerk in the employ of Messrs Cardwell & Co., in their cotton warehouse, Newmarket Buildings, Manchester, which employment he left about the end of 1828, and became a travelling canvasser for Pigot & Co.'s Manchester Directories. He was drowned while bathing in the river Thames, near Great Marlow, Bucks, on the 22d June 1829. He wrote "The Autobiography of William Charles Lovell," (himself,) and many poetical pieces in the local periodicals of the time, of Manchester, Liverpool, Whitby, &c. We select four of his songs from what he called the "Lyrics of the Heart."

### THE MOON IS BRIGHT.

Air—"*Row gently here, my Gondolier.*"

The moon is bright, the soft starlight
   Has gemm'd the silver stream ;
The silent flight of stars to-night,
   How beautiful they seem ;—
And all around is flung a power
   To charm the silent heart ;
The moon, stars, stream, dew, leaf, and flower,
   Proclaim how dear thou art.

The stream glides on, the moonlight's gone,
   The stars have died away ;
The leaves are strewn, flowers, one by one,
   Fade, wither, and decay.
But yet my love for thee is such,
   Time alters not my heart ;
And every change wrought by his touch
   But tells how dear thou art.

## MARGARET.

Artist's chisel could not trace
Such a form, with so much grace;
Never in Italian skies
Dwells such light as in her eyes.
Sweeter music ne'er was sung
Than hangs ever on her tongue;
Roses have not such a glow
As that upon her brilliant brow.
All that's bright and fair are met
In lovely, charming Margaret.

O'er her forehead, brightly fair,
Loosely floats her auburn hair,
Curl'd in ringlets with a flow,
Round a neck as white as snow;
Wild her eye as the gazelle's,
Where lurk love's ten thousand spells;
Fleet her step as woodland fawn,
Skipping o'er the dewy lawn;
In her every grace is met,
None may rival Margaret.

I will love her whilst her mind
Is pure and holy, good, refined,
Whilst such lovely glances fly
From the heaven of her eye;
Or pure feeling's ardent glow
Shines upon her open brow;
I should not be won unless
Her virtues match'd her loveliness.
On my heart a seal is set,
And on it graven—*Margaret.*

## REMEMBER ME.

REMEMBER me! remember me, when in the sapphire heaven
The stars have glanced, like ladies' eyes, upon the dews of even;
And glistening on each silver flower the dew has hung a gem,
Which dazzles like the diamonds in a kingly diadem.


Remember me! remember me, when in the western sky
Sunset has woven, of bright clouds, a crimson canopy,
And all her thousand golden hues sleep on the ocean's breast,
As slow and calm he sinks to sleep, like a monarch to his rest.

Remember me! remember me, when with the summer flowers
Thy fairy fingers form a wreath in beauty's brightest bowers;
And lingering round thy ruby lips is pleasure's brightest ray,
Oh! think how I would kiss those lips, if I were not away.

.    .    .    .    .    .

Remember me! remember me, when in thy prayers to Heaven,
Thy form just like a sculptured saint—thou pray'st to be forgiven;
Oh, mingle then my name with thine, as I shall do for thee;
At all these times—in all these things—lady, remember me!

## THE INVITATION.

Oh, come when the stars of heaven
    Are bright in their glorious home;
When the lingering stars of even
    Through gardens of emerald roam;
When the music that's flung from fountains
    Has a soft and magic tone,
And the moonlight sleeps on the mountains,
    Like dreams of flowers that are gone.

Oh, come when the night-dews glisten,
    And the star-beams glide on the sea,
And look from their thrones to listen
    The wave rolling joyous and free;
When on her rich couch beauty slumbers,
    Within her loveliest bower,
And music's wild thrilling numbers
    Float over each silvery flower.

Oh, come with thy beauty glowing,
    Thy bright dazzling eyes of blue,
Thy radiant locks wildly flowing,
    Round a neck of the purest hue;
With the noiseless foot of a fairy,
    Thine eyes sparkling wild with glee,
And thy form so light and airy,
    I pray thee, love, come to me.

## KITTY AN' ROBIN.

### SONG IN THE EAST LANCASHIRE DIALECT.

#### BY THE AUTHOR OF "SCARSDALE."

"WHEAR hast teh been roäming, Kitty?"
　"Oi'n nobbut been to th' well."
"Whear didst get yon posy, Kitty?"
　"Oi'n met wi' Robin Bell;
He wur sittin' top o' th' stele,
　Reet i' th' setting sun;
The dazzlin' glare it made me reel,
　Oi dropt my pail, an' run."

"An' what did Robin, Kitty?"
　"He chased me through the corn."
"Whear didst teh flee to, Kitty?"
　"Oi fell into a thorn.
Then Robin help'd me fro' the grund,
　He wur some koind fur sure;
An' nowt 'ud fit him till he fund
　This posy for my hure."

"What is gone wi' t' weyter, Kitty?"
　"Oh, Robin fill'd my pail."
"An' did he bring it whoam then, Kitty?"
　"Oh ay, how could he fail?
He said he'd fot it every neet,
　If yo'd bur let him come;
His wark is over whoile it's leet,
　An' he's noan far fro' whoam."

"How lang hast known o' Robin, Kitty?"
　"He's allus on yon stele."
"Whoi didst na tell thi mother, Kitty?"
　"Oi thowt yo'd known it weel.
He says he's addled fifty pund,
　An' bowt a kist an' clock;
He's ta'en a farm wi' gradely grund,
　His feyther'll foind the stock."

## MEG OR JENNY?

SONG IN THE EAST LANCASHIRE DIALECT.

BY THE AUTHOR OF "SCARSDALE."

WOE betoide the evil eye
    As smote eawr honest Jim,
He does nowt bur poine an' soigh;
    So what's amiss wi' him?
Alone thro' cloof and moor he'll roam,
    As tho' he were na' reet;
And oft he'll ma'e the heath his whoam
    Thro' all the starless neet.
        Is it Meg, or is it Jenny?
        Shall we brun owd Meg?
        Or, oh! wilt wed meh, Jenny?

Meg's hook-nosed, toothless, skinny,
    She's crook-back'd, hobbling, shrill;
What gowden hair has Jenny,
    Sweet rose o' Pendle Hill!
Her step is loike a roe's, that floies
    Up Sabden's sharpest pitch,
But beware her fatal eyes,
    The forest's pretty witch.
        Who's the witch, or Meg or Jenny?
        Shall we brun owd Meg?
        Or, oh! wilt wed meh, Jenny?

No forest hag with arts of hell,
    Had power like Jenny's eye,
To hold the heart as in a spell,
    Of love an' mystery.
Her dower is beauty, truth, an' grace,
    In gifts of nature rich,
There is no sorcery loike the face
    Of Pendle's latest witch.
        Who's the witch, or Meg or Jenny?
        Shall we brun owd Meg?
        Or, oh! wilt wed meh, Jenny?

Meet wi' bowder face her charm ;
　　Tell her yo' con match her art ;
Smoiles an' beauty work no harm ;
　　Nowt win boind bur heart wi' heart.
The spell 'at howds a soul whoile deäth,
　　Firm in danger's straitest hitch,
Is troth for troth wi' honour's breäth,
　　Of Pendle's sweetest witch !
　　　　Thae 'rt the witch, moi dearest Jenny,
　　　　Never brun owd Meg,
　　　　For theau wilt wed meh, Jenny.

## OH, WELL I LOVE MY GENTLE MAID.

### By J. B. Rogerson.

Oh, well I love my gentle maid,
　　For she is young and fair ;
Her eye is as the summer sky,
　　Like moon-clouds is her hair ;
Her voice is tuneful as a bird's,
　　Her step is light and free,
And better far than all besides,
　　She dearly loveth me.

I chose my love from out the crowd
　　Of beauty and of youth ;
I chose her for her loveliness,
　　I chose her for her truth ;
I never cease to bless that hour,
　　When first I chanced to see
The graceful and the beauteous one
　　Who dearly loveth me.

'Tis not amid a festive group
  My love doth seem most fair;
She best becomes the cheerful hearth,
  And well I love her there;
For, oh, 'twas in her quiet home—
  A maid's sweet sanctuary—
That first I won her sinless heart,
  And knew her love for me.


It may be wrong—I cannot brook
  That each rude eye should greet
The brightness of her fawn-like glance,
  Her form and features sweet;
Oh, no! I would that her dear charms
  Should all mine own charms be,
I would not lose one glance of hers
  Who dearly loveth me.


I do not think a wish of hers
  To others e'er can stray—
I know I am her dream by night,
  Her thought throughout the day;
But as the miser hides his gold,
  His soul's divinity,
So would I hide from eyes of man
  The maid who loveth me.

'Tis sweet to know a treasure mine,
  Which none besides can share;
'Tis sweet to think that beauty's lips
  Are moved for me in prayer;
'Tis sweet when she doth soothe my woe,
  Or light my hours of glee—
Oh, well I love the gentle maid,
  Who dearly loveth me.

## THE LOVER'S CALL.

(FROM "MISCELLANEOUS POEMS.")

### BY J. C. PRINCE.

OH ! when will the sweet spring come,
   With its sunshine, odours, and flowers,
And bring my beloved one home,
   To brighten the vernal hours ?
Like a worthless weed or a stone
   On the verge of the surging sea,
I am silent, and sad, and lone,
   Bereft of thy smiles and thee.

To the haunts where we used to rove,
   My loitering footsteps go,
Where I heard thy confession of love
   So tremulous, sweet, and low ;
But the rivulet seems to moan
   That thou art not also there,
And the trees send a plaintive tone,
   Like a sigh on the evening air.

I can find no charm in the day,
   No calm in the sombre night ;
Thou hast ta'en my repose away,
   And clouded the cheerful light :
To the heart that can love thee best
   Return, if still loyal to me ;
Come back, that my soul may rest,—
   I am weary waiting for thee.

## MY WYNDER.*

TUNE—*The rose-tree in full bearing.*

(FROM "HOMELY RHYMES," ETC.)

BY SAMUEL BAMFORD.

WHERE Gerrard's stream, with pearly gleam,
   Runs down in gay meander,
A weaver boy, bereft of joy,
   Upon a time did wander.
"Ah! well-a-day!" the youth did say,
   "I wish I did not mind her;
I'm sure had she regarded me,
   I ne'er had lost my wynder.

"Her ready hand was white as milk,
   Her fingers finely moulded,
And when she touch'd a thread of silk,
   Like magic it was folded.
She turn'd her wheel, she sang her song,
   And sometimes I have join'd* her:
Oh, that one strain would wake again
   From thee, my lovely wynder!

"And when the worsted hank she wound,
   Her skill was further proved;
No thread uneven there was found,
   Her bobbins never roved.
With sweet content, to work she went,
   And never look'd behind her,
With fretful eye, for ills to spy;
   But now I've lost my wynder.

---

\* In Lancashire pronounced *iined;* consequently a true rhyme to *wynder.*

† Finishing the weaving of a "cut," web, or piece.

"And never would she let me wait
 When downing † on a Friday;
Her wheel went at a merry rate,
 Her person always tidy.
But she is gone, and I'm alone;
 I know not where to find her;
I've sought the hill, the wood and rill;
 No tidings of my wynder.

"I've sought her at the dawn of day,
 I've sought her at the noonin';
I've sought her when the evening gray
 Had brought the hollow moon in.

I've call'd her on the darkest night,
 With wizard spells to bind her;
And when the stars arose in light,
 I've wander'd forth to find her.

"Her hair was like the raven's plume,
 And hung in tresses bonny;
Her cheeks so fair did roses bear,
 That blush'd as sweet as ony.
With slender waist, and carriage chaste,
 Her looks were daily kinder,
I mourn and rave, and cannot weave
 Since I have lost my wynder.

## CANZONETTE.

### By J. B. Rogerson.

There is a place where the forest boughs
    Bend down to a quiet stream,
And so lovely it looks in its bright repose,
    That it seems as 'twere wrapt in a dream;
The water-lily uplifts its head
    In that sweet and pleasant home,
Like a living pearl in a silver bed,
    Or a bell of the wave's white foam;
There comes not a sound on the passing air,
    Save the young birds' cheerful call—
Beloved one! wilt thou meet me there,
    When the shadows of even fall?

There is a bower on that peaceful spot,
    Which some fond hand hath wrought,
Where the feet of the worldling enter not,
    Sacred to love and thought;
Full many fair flowers beside it sigh,
    And the myrtle around it creeps,
The breeze becomes sweet as it floateth by,
    And the bee in its roses sleeps;
The stars alone will our secrets share,
    Unseen and unheard by all—
Beloved one! wilt thou meet me there
    When the shadows of even fall?

## SHE'S NOT SO FAIR.

### BY CHARLES SWAIN.

SHE'S not so fair as many there,
   But she's as loved as any,
And few you'll find with such a mind,
   Or such a heart, as Nannie:
A maiden grace, a modest face,
   A smile to win us ever;
And she has sense, without pretence—
   She's good as she is clever!

She's not so fine as some may shine,
   With feathers, pearls, and laces;
But oh, she's got, what they have not,
   With all their borrow'd graces,—
Eyes blue and bright with heaven's light,
   That kindle with devotion;
A cheek of rose, a heart that glows
   With every sweet emotion!
      She's not so fair, &c.

## MY JOHNNY.

### By R. R. Bealey.

My Johnny is the bonniest lad
   'Ut lives i' Rachda' town—
His een are blue, his cheeks are red,
   His curly yure is brown.
He walks just like a gentleman—
   And that's just what he'll be;
Aw like to walk about wi' him,
   An' let o th' neighbours see.


An' then he's gettin' larnt i' books,
   An' reads o th' pappers too;
And when he comes a courtin' me
   He tells me all 'ut's new.
He sends a letter now and then,
   An' writes outside it—" Miss ;"
An' as it comes instead of John,
   It allus gets a kiss.


He warks i' the factory, an' if those
   'Ut wear his wark but knew
What sort o' chap the weyver wur,
   They'd love it same's aw do.
They'd nobbut wear 't in better days,
   Then lay it nicely by;
John mixes love wi' everything,
   An' ma'es bread taste like pie.


On Sunday when aw goo to church,
   An' get set nicely down,
Aw never know what th' parson says,
   My heart's i' Rachda' town.
But Johnny comes i' th' afternoon,
   An' never speaks in vain;
Aw swallow every word he says,
   Like thirsty flowers drink rain.


Aw like to yer at th' cookoo sing,
   I' weepin' April's days;
Aw like to look at the layrock rise,
   An' scatter down his praise.

Aw like to stand i' th' quiet lone,
    While dayleet passes by;
But more by the hauve nor these, aw like
    To yer my Johnny sigh.

Oh happy me, oh lucky me,
    To have a chap like John;
He says aw 'm th' nicest lass i' th' world,
    Aw 'm sure he's th' finest mon.
He hasn't got a single fau't,
    An's fur too good for me;
But since my Johnny loves me so,
    My very best aw'll be.

He says he's puttin' money by,
    To get a heawse for me;
An' when he's gotten brass enough,
    He says we wed mun be.
Aw dunnot like to think o' that,
    An' yet it's gradely true:
To be John's sweetheart o my life
    Aw think 'ud hardly do.

## BERTHA.

### By Henry Kirk, of Goosnargh.

Low, by Ribble's scaury side,
    Swept the soft, autumnal breeze;
Faint its whisp'ring murmurs died,
    High in Tonbrook's crowded trees.
Sad, at intervals, the grove
    Shook beneath a fitful blast;
Like a heart that vainly strove
    Back to crush some sorrow past!

Bertha came not to the seat
    Of our fonder, earlier faith;
False the heart that was to beat
    Constant, truthful, e'en to death!
Bertha, little did I deem
    Thou couldst thus inconstant be,
Warm as still thy vows would seem,
    Plighted in that grove to me!

## TO MARY.

### BY JOHN HARLAND F.S.A.

As the thirsty desert-wanderer seeks the oasis green
    and fair;
As for pardon seeks the penitent, with tears and fer-
    vent prayer;
As youth seeks fame, and age seeks rest, and the life-
    sick look above;
As all in hope seek happiness,—so have I sought thy
    love.

With blushes mantling on thy cheek, with modesty
    and grace,
With tears and smiles alternating upon thy lovely
    face;
With murmurings soft and sweeter far than music of
    the grove,
With faith and trust and purity,—thou gavest me thy
    love.

As misers guard their golden god—as maidens prize
    their fame—
As honest men would keep through life a pure and
    spotless name—
As hope is held to wretched hearts—as pity shields the
    dove—
So I guard, I prize, I hold, I keep, thy pure and price-
    less love.

Than radiant light more lustrous, than life itself more
    dear;
Richer than all the riches of this transitory sphere;
Outliving change and death, in eternity above—
This has been—Mary! this is now,—this e'er shall be,
    our love.

## COME, LOVE, AND SING.

### BY J. B. ROGERSON.

COME, love, and sing, in thy tones sweet and low,
The song which I heard from thy lips long ago,
When thine eyes were as bright, and thy cheeks were as fair
As the hues which the skies and the summer flowers wear,
And vainly I strove with my kisses to chase
The pure stream of blushes that rush'd o'er thy face.

Come, sing me that song, love, 'twill bring back the day,
When my heart was lit up by Affection's first ray;
When thy name to mine ears was a sound of delight,
And I gazed on thine image in dreams of the night,
And arose, when the sky wore the morning's bright beam,
But to muse on the eyes that had shone in my dream.

Then sing me that song, love; for oh, with each tone
There will come back the thoughts of the hours that are gone—
Of the love that had birth amid blushes and fears,
Yet hath lived through the tempest of trouble and tears;
Oh! that time will come back of deep rapture and pride,
When I woo'd thee and won thee, my beautiful bride!

## SERENADE.

### By William Mort.

I WILL come to thee, love, when the bright stars are shining,
And the weary old moon in her course is declining,—
With a fond mother's thought slowly stealing away,
That her children may join unrestrain'd in their play!
    I will come.

I will come to thee, love, when night's mantle is spread
O'er the earth, like a shroud that envelops the dead—
Making hallow'd a scene which might else from thy breast
Scare the innocent thoughts that had there taken rest!
    I will come.

I will come to thee, love, when the birds are all sleeping,
And silence barefooted o'er nature is creeping;
When the trees are quite still, and the winds hold their breath,
Lest a leaflet disturb the hush'd quiet beneath!
    I will come.

I will come to thee, love, and the morrow shall find us
In a world of our own, where no shackles may bind us;
I will come, love, ere yet the stars shrink from the skies,
And my guerdon shall be the sweet thanks of thine eyes!
    I will come—I will come!

## WE MET.

### By Henry Kirk.

We met, as only two can meet,
    Whose eyes flash mutual fire;
Greeted, as only two can greet,
    When words in sighs expire.

We stray'd, as only two can stray,
    Whose confidence is sure;
We play'd, as only two can play,
    Whose innocence is pure.

We praised, as only two can praise,
    That fear no flatteries;
Embraced, as only two embrace,
    Ere evil passions rise.

We felt, as only two can feel,
    Whom equal wishes guide;
Reveal'd, what only two reveal,
    Who mutual trust confide.

We loved, as only two can love,
    That know no fear or guile;
We've proved, as only two can prove,
    That doubt each fear and smile.

We own, with those, the vacant heart,
    That find their love in vain;
We part, as only two can part,
    That ne'er may meet again!

## I'LL TELL MY MOTHER.

### By J. B. Rogerson.

Timid little Marian,
  With her blooming beauty,
In an instant lured me
  From the path of duty;
Nothing else I thought of,
  Nothing, and no other;
Though she cried, if I but touch'd her,—
  "Don't!—I'll tell my mother!"

When she heard me coming,
  Straight she sought some hiding,
And broke out in laughter,
  Checking thus my chiding;
If I did but press her hand
  More warmly than a brother,
She said, and snatch'd her fingers,
  "Don't!—I'll tell my mother!"

When the love I bore her
  Could not be dissembled,
And our lips encounter'd,
  How she blush'd and trembled!
That *one* kiss she forgave me,
  But, when I stole another,
She cried out, yet not loudly,
  "Oh!—I'll tell my mother!"

Mine, I said, she must be,
  Without more denying;
For all night I slept not,
  And all day was sighing;
She must answer me with "Yes!"
  That *one word*, and no other;
She only sigh'd and whisper'd,
  "Pray don't tell my mother!"

## TH' SWEETHEART GATE.

### By Edwin Waugh.

Air—"*The Manchester Angel.*"

Oh, there's mony a gate eawt ov eawr teawn-end,—
   But nobbut one for me;
It winds by a rindlin' wayter side,
   An' o'er a posied lea:
It wanders into a shady dell;
   An' when aw ve done for th' day,
Oh, aw never can sattle this heart o' mine,
   Beawt walkin' deawn that way.

It's noather garden, nor posied lea,
   Nor wayter rindlin' clear;
But deawn i' th' vale there's a rosy nook,
   An' my true love lives theer.
It's olez summer wheer th' heart's content,
   Tho' wintry winds may blow;
An' theer's never a gate 'at's so kind to th' fuut,
   As th' gate cne likes to go.

When aw set off o' sweetheartin', aw've
   A theawsan' things to say;
But th' very first glent o' yon chimbley-top,
   It drives 'em o away;
An' when aw meet wi' my bonny lass,
   It sets my heart a-jee;—
Oh, there's summut i' th' leet o' yon two blue een
   That plays the dule wi' me!

When th' layrock's finish'd his wark aboon,
   An' laid his music by,
He flutters deawn to his mate, an' stops
   Till dayleet stirs i' th' sky.
Though Matty sends me away at dark,
   Aw know that hoo's reet full well;—
An' it's heaw aw love a true-hearted lass,
   No mortal tung can tell.

Aw wish that Candlemas day were past,
   When wakin' time comes on;
An' aw wish that Kesmas time were here,
   An' Matty an' me were one.
Aw wish this wanderin' wark were o'er—
   This maunderin' to an' fro;
That aw could go whoam to my own true love,
   An' stop at neet an' o.

## THE LOVED AND LOST.

### By Henry Kirk.

The grass waves green above the tomb,
    Where dark in death young Ellen lies;
No more shall pleasure scare the gloom
        From Richard's eyes!

Oh, better far the love, where Death
    Hath set the seal no time destroys,
Than that, which on some wanton's breath
        Hath placed its joys!

Still lives that love, unchanged and bright,
    Fresh blooming each successive year;
No jealous pangs—no doubts to blight;
        No wrongs to fear!

Then clear thy brow; for she, my friend,
    Thy angel-wife, thy heart's true love,
Shall point, in life's uncertain end,
        Thy path above!

The world has claims 'twere wrong to shun
    For one so young. Some other heart
As full of mirth may yet be won,
        And bliss impart!

Life is not such a bitter thing
    As fools believe, in idiot madness;
'Tis our own thoughts and actions bring
        Our woe or gladness.

Then learn to live, and cultivate
    The warmer feelings of the soul;
Fly empty follies, ere "too late"
        Thy reason call!

## LOVELY SUSANNAH.

(FROM "THE THUNDERSTORM— A RURAL SKETCH.")

### By Thomas Nicholson.*

LOVELY Susannah's away to the wood;
   Lonely and musing, and moody goes she:
Yes, she goes all alone; but she is good,
   And loves the sweet woodlark that sings in the tree.

Lovely Susannah has gone through the glade:
   Hath not a coy maiden some danger to fear
So deep in the wood? She loves best the shade,
   And the ringdove's complaint is sweet to her ear.

Hark, a shrill whistle! She turns not away—
   No, fearless Susannah still onward doth move;
Yet, that's not the woodlark tuning his lay,
   Nor yet the soft plaint of the mild-cooing dove.

'Twas not the ringdove that kept her so long;
   Nor was it the woodlark's wild music so clear;
Oh, no! 'twas a softer, a much sweeter song,
   More pleasing by far to a fond maiden's ear!

Oh, say not she knew that young Edwin was there:
   No bird's note loved he like the woodlark's sweet strain,
And the ringdove's soft coo. How like were the pair!
   'Twas accident brought them together, 'tis plain!

---

\* The author, who published his little volume at 63 Berkeley Street, Strangeways, Manchester, says, "I neither make a boast of poverty nor desire riches."

## MAGGIE.

### By Richard R. Bealey.

Oh, thou bonny rose-lipp'd lassie,
   More than roses thou must be;
For the month of rosy beauty
   Is but March compared with thee—
      My love Maggie,
         Sweetheart Maggie,
   All the flowers thou art to me.

Yet the flowers of field or garden,
   Breathing fragrance on the breeze;
Or the birds that carol sweetly,
   Making concert in the trees;
      My love Maggie,
         Sweetheart Maggie,
   These have not thy power to please.

My poor heart was cold and barren,
   Cold as winter, and as drear,
Until thou, by smiling on me,
   Gavest me summer all the year;
      My love Maggie,
         Sweetheart Maggie,
   Flowers must bloom when thou art near.

Summer-time, and spring, and autumn,
   All their mantles o'er thee fling;
Laureate art thou to the seasons,
   Praising, loving everything;
      My love Maggie,
         Sweetheart Maggie,
   Queen thou art; oh, make me King!

## BETTER THAN BEAUTY.

### By Charles Swain.

My love is not a beauty
    To other eyes than mine;
Her curls are not the fairest,
    Her eyes are not divine:
Nor yet like rose-buds parted,
    Her lips of love may be;
But though she's not a beauty,
    She's dear as one to me.

Her neck is far from swan-like,
    Her bosom unlike snow;
Nor walks she like a deity
    This breathing world below:
Yet there's a light of happiness
    Within, which all may see;
And though she's not a beauty,
    She's dear as one to me.

I would not give the kindness,
    The grace that dwells in *her*,
For all that Cupid's blindness
    In others might prefer!
I would not change *her* sweetness
    For pearls of any sea;
For better far than beauty
    Is one *kind heart* to me.

## NOTHING MORE.

### By John Bolton Rogerson.

In a valley fair I wander'd,
   O'er its meadow pathways green,
Where a singing brook was flowing,
   Like the spirit of the scene;
And I saw a lovely maiden,
   With a basket brimming o'er
With sweet buds, and so I ask'd her
   For a flower, and nothing more.

Then I chatted on beside her,
   And I praised her hair and eyes,
And, like roses from her basket,
   On her cheeks saw blushes rise;
With her timid looks down glancing,
   She said, "Would I pass before?"
But I said that all I wanted
   Was a smile, and nothing more.

So she slyly smiled upon me,
   And I still kept wandering on;
What with blushing, smiling, chatting,
   Soon a brief half-hour was gone.
Then she told me I must leave her,
   For she saw their cottage door;
But I would not till I rifled
   Just a kiss, and nothing more.

And I often met that maiden
   At the twilight's loving hour,
With the summer's offspring laden,
   But herself the dearest flower.
When she ask'd me what I wish'd for,
   Grown far bolder than before,
With impassion'd words I answer'd,
   'Twas her heart, and nothing more.

Thus for weeks and months I woo'd her,
   And the joys that then had birth,
Made an atmosphere of gladness
   Seem encircling all the earth.
One bright morning at the altar
   A white bridal dress she wore;
Then my wife I proudly made her,
   And I ask for nothing more!

## NUPTIAL LINES.

WRITTEN ON THE OCCASION OF THE MARRIAGE OF THE HON. LADY ELIZABETH GREY DE WILTON WITH THE HON. CAPTAIN DUDLEY CHARLES DE ROS, AT PRESTWICH.

BY GEORGE RICHARDSON,
*Author of "Patriotism," &c., &c.*

CHORUS.

Hark, the merry bells are ringing!
Festive joy and homage bringing;
And village-friends keep holiday—
The bridal-morn of Lady Grey.

MANY a banner high is streaming,
Glad eyes fervent pleasure beaming;
Lo! the happy train advances—
Bridal-maids with smiling glances.
   Hark, &c.

'Tis past—the sacred plighted vow!
Dear lady, free from care as now—
May virtue, truth, and honour prove,
Thy early dreams of wedded love.
   Hark, &c.

Tender damsels odours bringing,
On thy path gay flowers are flinging;
Clad like vestals in pure whiteness,
Dropping sunny bloom and brightness.
   Hark, &c.

May the beauteous offering be
A type of blessed years for thee!
And life a chalice of rich treasure,
Ever fill'd with love's sweet measure!

  Hark, the merry bells are ringing!
  Booming guns are pleasure winging;
  And villagers keep holiday—
  For gentle, happy Lady Grey.

## "I GAZED O'ER THE BLUE STILL WATERS."

### By James Horton Groves.*

I gazed o'er the blue, still waters wide,
    As the morn was nodding gray,
Expecting a homeward sail to glide,
    From a land beyond the sea.
But the sun rose high, and again sunk low,
    And no sail appear'd to view;
Oh! I sigh'd, as the wind began to blow,
    For my absent sailor true.

I gazed on the troubled waters wide,
    Till the sun rose to his height;
I watch'd the ebb and the flow of the tide,
    E'en till the approach of night.
But no sail appear'd my soul to cheer,
    And the waves more fiercely drove;
As the tempest rose, I sigh'd with fear
    For my absent sailor love.

I still gazed over the rough, wide sea,
    And aloud began to weep;
And just as the darkness veil'd the day,
    I closed my eyes in sleep;
And I thought that an angel clasp'd me round,
    And kiss'd me as I mourn'd;
I awoke—and myself in the arms I found
    Of my sailor true, return'd!

---

* A Manchester rhymester, who published, some years ago, by subscription, a thin volume of Poems, &c., including a Drama in three acts, called, "M'Alpine; or, The Warlock Chieftain."

## BUT I AM SAD.

### By R. R. Bealey.

The summer-time is full of flowers,
  The gardens all are gay,
They breathe the sunshine, drink the showers,
  And laugh the hours away.
The trees are clad in robes of green,
  And birds among them sing;
But I am sad, and can't be glad—
  My joy has ta'en the wing.

The brooks and rivers run along,
  With music to the sea;
The willows kiss them for their song,
  The breezes join the glee.
The joyous clouds together play,
  Or chase each other on;
But I am sad, and can't be glad—
  My happy days are gone.

I used to love the summer-time,
  I used to love the spring;
But since my love has proved untrue,
  No joy to me they bring.
It seems as if the winter time,
  Had crept o'er all the year;
It's very cold within my heart—
  It's very dark and drear.

Oh, heart of mine with blighted love,
  What power thy life can save?
I'm like a yew tree, dark and sad,
  Beside an open grave.
My love I call both loud and long,
  And in my tears I cry,
But, No! he'll never love me more,
  And love-less I must die.

## "OH, MIRK AND STORMY."

(FROM "THE WILD FLOWERS OF POETRY.") *

### By James Horton Groves.

" Oh, mirk and stormy is the nicht ;
   So ope the door and let me ben ;
Unto my sark I'm dripping weet,
   An' a' my body's stiffenen'.
For sake o' thee, my bonnie lass,
   I cam' through storm o' hail an' snaw,
An' ay agen for thee I'd pass
   A storm, to hae a kiss or twa."

" I'm sorry that ye hither cam',
   I daur na let ye ben, my joe ;
Our auld folks are awa' frae hame ;
   To do so wad be sin, ye know.
An' though ye cam' through snaw an' hail,
   To let ye ben wad be my wrang ;
Nor tempt me, gif ye wish me hale ;
   So back again, my laddie, gang."

" I wish ye hale, ye know it too ;
   But deep the snaw is driftin' fast ;
I may be buried in a slough,
   Or perish in the bitin' blast,—
Then wad ye wish ye'd let me stay ;
   Then wad ye wish ye'd oped the door ;
When, stretch'd a corse, ye see me lay,
   Na mair to luve, or kiss ye mair."

---

\* "The work," says the writer, "of a poor, self-taught, young man."

"Talk na sae woefu',—me ye fright;
   I wadna now ye went till day;
Could ye na mak' a shift the nicht
   To lie i' th' barn amang the hay?
For hark! the owlet's screeching din,
   It bodes o' strife, an' wad ye warn;
The warlock, too, now haunts the glen,
   So tarry, pray ye, in the barn."


"I care na for the owlet's din;
   I care na for the warlock's strife;
Gif ye'll na gladly let me ben,
   I care na either for my life.
Nor storm, nor snaw, whate'er's my lot,
   Shall tempt me in your barn to stay;
An' gif ye keep me out o' th' cot,
   The gate I cam' I'll back away."


"Nay, gae na back; 'tis na my will!
   Come ben, an' shelter frae the storm;
The ragin' blast is cauld an' chill;
   Our bleezin' ingle's cheerin' warm.
I meant na what I said, my dear;
   So doff your clothes, I'll dry them weel;
Then sit ye down in th' elbow'd chair,
   An' drive the cauld wi' th' gudeman's ale"


"Thy ruddy lips oh let me taste,
   Like simmer roses weet wi' dew;
An' o' the sweetness let me feast,
   Issuin' frae thy bonnie mou'.
An' then the gudeman's ale I'll try,
   Na hauf sae sparklin' as thine ee;
Nor in the barn on hay I'll lie,
   But sit, my luve, beside o' thee!"

## "IN A SNUG LITTLE NOOK."

### By Thomas Brierley.*

In a snug little nook, by a rippling brook,
    'Tis there that my true love dwells;
'Tis shaded with trees, and fann'd by the breeze,
    And laden with witching spells.
There, there I recline 'neath the sweet woodbine,
    And marlock† her raven hair,
I clasp her fingers where beauty lingers,
    And we bask in the rosy air.
        Then here's to the cot, the neat little cot,
            Where my true love resides;
        May it contain love's rosy chain,
            And a fountain of pleasure-tides!

I ponder and stare in the starry fair,
    That's held in the heavens at night,
And wonder what arm, with its mighty charm,
    Could have made such stellar light.
And betimes I dream of a sunny sheen,
    Too glitt'ring for earthly birth,
And there I woo, 'mid the balmy dew,
    This beautiful nymph of earth.
        Then here's to the cot, the neat little cot,
            Where my true love resides;
        May it contain love's rosy chain,
            And a fountain of pleasure-tides!

---

\* The writer is a silk-weaver at Alkrington, near Middleton; and author of "Th' Silk-Weaver's Fust Bearin'-home," and other tales, &c.
† Play with.

## THE ARDENT LOVER.

BY THE LATE EDWARD RUSHTON, of Liverpool.*

Ah, Mary! by that feeling mind,
Improved by thought, by taste refined,
And by those blue bewitching eyes,
And by those soul-seducing sighs,
And by that cheek's delicious bloom,
And by those lips that breathe perfume,
Here do I bow at Beauty's shrine,
And pledge this glowing heart of mine.

The tame, the impotent of soul,
A haughty mandate may control,
May make him slight a Helen's charms,
And take a dowdy to his arms;
But when did dark maternal schemes,
Or the stern father's towering dreams,
Or when did power or affluence, move
The heart sublimed by real love?

The cold, slow thing that tamely woos,
Just as his worldly friends may choose,
Is but a snail on beauty's rose,
That crawls and soils where'er he goes.
Not so the youth whose mantling veins
Are fill'd with love's ecstatic pains;
He heeds nor gold, nor craft, nor pride,
But strains, all nerve, his blushing bride.

Come, then, oh! come, and let me find
A pleader in thy feeling mind,
And let the beams from those blue eyes
Disperse the clouds that round me rise;
And let those lips that breathe perfume,
With speed pronounce my blissful doom,
With speed before the sacred shrine
Pledge thy dear self for ever mine.

## THE LANCASHIRE WITCH.

### By the late John Scholes.

An owd maid aw shall be, for aw'm eighteen to-morn,
   An' aw m'yen to keep sengle an' free;
But the dule's i' the lads, for a plague they were born,
   An' thi' never con let one a-be, a-be,
   They never con let one a-be.

Folk seyn aw'm to' pratty to dee an owd maid,
   An' 'at luv' sits an' laughs i' my ee;
By-leddy! aw'm capt' 'at folk wantin' to wed;
   Thi' mey o tarry sengle for me, for me,
   Thi' mey o tarry sengle for me.

There's Robin a' Mill,—he's so fond of his brass,—
   Thinks to bargain like shoddy for me;
He may see a foo's face if he looks in his glass,
   An' aw'd thank him to let me a-be, a-be,
   Aw'd thank him to let me a-be.

Coom a chap t'other day o i' hallidi' trim,
   An' he swoor he'd goo dreawn him for me;
"Hie thi whoam furst an' doff thi," aw sed, "bonny Jim!
   Or thae'll spuyl a good shute, does-ta see, does-ta see,
   Thae'll spuyl a good shute, does-ta see."

Cousin Dick says aw've heawses, an' land, an' some gowd,
   An' he's plann'd it so weel, dun yo' see!
When we're wed he'll ha' th' heawses new-fettled an' sowd,
   But aw think he may let um a-be, a-be,
   Sly Dicky may let um a-be.

Ned's just volunteer'd into th' "roifle recruits,"
   An' a dashin' young sodiur is he;
If his gun's like his een, it'll kill wheer it shoots,
   But aw'll mind as they dunnot shoot me, shoot me,
   Aw'll mind as they dunnot shoot me.

He sidles i' th' lone, an' he frimbles at th' yate,
   An' he comes as he coom no' for me;
He spers for eawr John, bo' says nought abeawt Kate,
   An' just gi'es a glent wi' his ee, his ee,
   An' just gi'es a glent wi' his ee.

He's tall an' he's straight, an' his curls are like gowd,
   An' there's summat so sweet in his ee,
'At aw think i' my heart, if he'd nobbut be bowd,
   He needna' quite let me a-be, a-be,
   He needna' quite let me a-be.

## TH' HEART-BROKKEN.

By John Higson, of Droylsden.*

Mi honds un mi faze ur' quoite ceawd,
Aw'm weet-shurt and weet to my skin,
Wor pluff stilts they slid fro' mi grip,
Bur it's neawt toart what's ailin' within.

Aw care no' fo' weet nur fo' rain,
Nur th' woind os it coms o'er yon broo;
Bur aw'm thinkin' o' Meary, sweet lass,
Till mi heart iz fair brokken i' two.

Laast neet fur to meet her u'th' steel,
Aw crop deawn mi way e o' crack,
Os soon os aw'd suppert mi ceaws,
Un' filt mi tit's mannger un' rack.

Aw shackert un' waytud till ten,
Bu' Meary ne'er awst furt' com eawt;
Ut last aw gan t' whissle ut durr,
When ther Sam he coom preawin' abeawt.

Aw axt him iv Moll wur i' th' heawse;
"Yigh, yigh, bur hoo's noan wantin' thee,
Fur a chap 'ut's wuth plenty o' braass,
Hus bin bur just neaw her furt' see.

Iv o' Sunday to't chourch theaw wilt gang,
Ther axins tha'll yer um coed o'er;
So tha'st no cageon ston' hanklin' theere,
Fur Meary 'ull sithi no moor."

Os he slamm'd i' mi faze cottage durr,
He laaft e his sleighve, did ther Sam,—
Aw con stond to be byetten reet weel,
Bur aw conno' the'r jaw un' the'r gam'.

Aw've pur up wi' mich i' this wo'ld,
Aw've fou't weel it' battle o' loife,
Bur aw ne'er wur so done up ofore,
Os e lozin' mi chance ov o woife.

Mi heart, mon, 's fair riven i' two,
Aw'st ne'er ha' no pleshur aw'm shure;
So aw'll run mi cunthri un' place,
Un' never com nar 'um no moor.

---

* Author of the "Gorton Historical Recorder," "Historical and Descriptive Notices of Droylsden," &c.

## THE DOMINIE'S COURTSHIP.

### By Robert Rockliff.

He woo'd her in the wisest way
    That woman may be woo'd
By any pedagogue, who is
    In a conjunctive mood;
For in a studied speech, replete
    With academic learning,
He pour'd into her ear the love
    With which his heart was yearning.


" Dear Emma!" he exclaimed, "if I
    Could win thee for my wife—
A helpmate unto me through all
    The *accidence* of life,
My *sum* of happiness would be
    Complete with this *addition;*
For even should we *multiply,*
    We'd live without *division.*


"Thy beauty is *superlative,*
    So matchless in *degree,*
That maids of every *form* and *class*
    Must all *give place* to thee.
The finest *figure* of them all,
    If scrutinised with rigour,
Would prove a *cypher* at thy side,
    And make, in fact, no *figure.*


"Thy grace, too, is the general *theme,*
    For in thy walk is seen
A *style* of carriage, that might be
    A *copy* for a queen;
In fact, thy charms are such that, like
    The *ruler* of the nation,
Thy presence everywhere is hail'd
    With *notes of admiration!*

"I have not much to offer thee
    Beyond my heart and hand,
But every *article* I have
    Shall be at thy command.
Oh! pity, then, my hapless *case*,
    And look with condescension,
On one whose passion hath endured
    For years without *declension*."

How could an artless maid resist
    A Bachelor of Arts,
Who even in his *parts of speech*
    Show'd such uncommon parts?
Their hands were join'd, and ever since
    That happy *conjugation*,
The *term* of his domestic life
    Has been one *long vacation!*

---

## BERTHA.

### By Henry Kirk, of Goosnargh.

Low, by Ribble's scaury side,
    Swept the soft, autumnal breeze;
Faint its whisp'ring murmurs died,
    High in Tonbrook's crowded trees.
Sad, at intervals, the grove
    Shook beneath a fitful blast;
Like a heart that vainly strove
    Back to crush some sorrow past!

Bertha came not to the seat
    Of our fonder, earlier faith;
False the heart that was to beat
    Constant, truthful, e'en to death!
Bertha, little did I deem
    Thou couldst thus inconstant be,
Warm as still thy vows would seem,
    Plighted in that grove to me!

III.

## Songs of Home and its Affections.

### IT IS BUT A COTTAGE.

#### By Charles Swain.

It is but a cottage, but where is the heart
   That would love not its home, be it ever so small?
There's a charm in the spot which no words may impart,
   Where the birds and the roses seem sweetest of all.

It is but a cottage, but still for a friend
   There's a chair and whatever the table supplies.
To the mind that's content with what fortune may send,
   Why, a cot is a palace that monarchs may prize.

I envy no statesman his honours and fame;
   The path of ambition is deck'd to ensnare;
The title most dear is a good honest name,
   And ambition may envy the man without care.

It is but a cottage, a slight little place,
   Scarce worthy the glance of a traveller's eyes;
But, oh! with content, and a friend's smiling face,
   Why, a cot is a palace that monarchs might prize.

## THE PLEASURES O' WHOAM.

From "Phases of Distress—Lancashire Rhymes."

### By Joseph Ramsbottom.

This faggin' on, this wastin' sthrife,
    This drudgin' wark, wi' scanty fare,
This cheattin' dyeath 'at we co'n life,
    Wi' ev'ry comfort dasht wi' care.
To ate an' sleep, to fret an' slave,
    I' this breet warld o' sun an' fleawrs,—
If this wur' o poor men could have,
    They'd weary soon o' th' bitter heawrs.

. . . . . .

At th' eend o' th' day, mi wark o done,
    An' quite content, aw'm sat at whoam,
Mi childher brimmin' o'er wi' fun,
    'Ull singin' reawnd abeawt me come.
An' th' young'st 'ull romp up on mi knee,
    An' th' next between my legs 'ull get,
An' th' owdest in his cheer 'ull be
    Hutcht close as it con weel be set.

What merry laughs, what lispins then,
    O' wondhrous things they'n chanced to see;
What kissins reawnd an' reawnd agen!
    It's busy wark to mind o three:
What flingin' arms abeawt mi neck,
    What passin' fingers thro' mi yure,
What neighsy fun witheawt a check,
    What rowlin' o'er an' o'er o' th' flure!

An' th' wife looks on wi' glist'nin' ee,
    An smile 'ut dhrives o care away;
Heaw preawd hoo feels, it's plain to see,
    I' watchin' th' childher romp an' play.
When sleep is sattlin' on their lids,
    An' oitch begins to nod its yed,
O reawnd agen aw kiss mi brids,
    Afore hoo packs 'em off to bed.

An' tho' eawr crust be hard an' bare;
   Tho' petches on eawr dress be seen;
An' th' sky hang black wi cleawds o' care,
   Wi' hardly one blue rent between;
Tho' th' rich o' life's good things han moore,
   They'v noan as mony scenes like this;
Thus heaven i' kindness gi'es to th' poor
   No scanty foretaste of its bliss.

## FAREWELL TO MY COTTAGE.

WRITTEN ON LEAVING BLACKLEY TO LIVE IN LONDON.

### By Samuel Bamford.

FAREWELL to my cottage that stands on the hill,
To valleys and fields where I wander'd at will,
And met early spring with her buskin of dew,
As o'er the wild heather a joyance she threw;
'Mid fitful sun-beamings, with bosom snow-fair,
And showers in the gleamings, and wind-beaten hair,
She smiled on my cottage, and buddings of green
On elder and hawthorn and woodbine were seen,—
The crocus came forth with its lilac and gold,
And fair maiden snowdrop stood pale in the cold,—
The primrose peep'd coyly from under the thorn,
And blithe look'd my cottage on that happy morn.
But spring pass'd away, and the pleasure was o'er,
And I left my dear cottage to claim it no more.
Farewell to my cottage—afar must I roam—
No longer a cottage, no longer a home.

For bread must be earn'd, though my cot I resign,
Since what I enjoy shall with honour be mine;
So up to the great city I must depart,
With boding of mind and a pang at my heart.
Here all seemeth strange, as if foreign the land,
A place and a people I don't understand;
And as from the latter I turn me away,
I think of old neighbours, now lost, well-a-day!
I think of my cottage full many a time,
A nest among flowers at midsummer prime;

With sweet pink, and white rock, and bonny rose bower,
And honey-bine garland o'er window and door;
As prim as a bride ere the revels begin,
And white as a lily without and within.
Could I but have tarried, contented I'd been,
Nor envied the palace of "Lady the Queen."
And oft at my gate happy children would play,
Or sent on an errand well pleasèd were they,—
A pitcher of water to fetch from the spring,
Or wind-broken wood from my garden to bring;
On any commission they'd hasten with glee,
Delighted when serving dear Ima,* or me,—
For I was their "uncle," and "gronny" was she.
And then as a recompense, sure if not soon,
They'd get a sweet posy on Sunday forenoon,
Or handful of fruit would their willing hearts cheer.
I miss the dear children,—none like them are here,
Though offspring as lovely as mother e'er bore,
At eve in the Park I can count by the score.
But these are not ours,—of a stranger they're shy,
So I can but bless them as passing them by;
When ceasing their play, my emotion to scan,
I dare say they wonder "what moves the old man."

Of ours, some have gone in their white coffin shroud,
And some have been lost in the world and its crowd;
One only remains, the last bird in the nest—
Our own little grandchild,† the dearest and best.
But vain to regret, though we cannot subdue
The feelings to nature and sympathy true;
Endurance, with patience, must bear the strong part,—
Sustain, when they cannot give peace to, the heart;
Till life with its yearnings and struggles is o'er,
And I shall remember my cottage no more.

---

\* A diminutive of Jemima, the Christian name of the poet's wife.
† The child of a neighbour, who called the author and his wife "grondad" and "gronny."

## EARLY HAUNTS VISITED.

### By R. W. Procter.*

When childhood, fairy boon from fate,
    Wreath'd smiles upon my brow,
I press'd this dear, familiar spot,
    Where beauty reign'd as now.
Each field and flower gave forth its bloom,
    Each light and sunny thing
Rejoiced with me, while wandering free,
    Bless'd children of the spring!

How many years have noiseless sped
    Since last I saw this glen,—
How oft by fierce commotions torn
    Yon world of busy men,—
How much of change this heart has known,
    Of hopes, of smiles, of tears,—
Yet o'er this sweet and lone retreat
    No trace of time appears.

Thus, when the sun's all-glorious beams
    Have vanquish'd winter's gloom,
Blithe nature wakes again to life,
    Triumphant o'er the tomb;
'Tis thus the simplest leaves and flowers,
    With weeds, that meanly grow,
Enjoy perpetual bloom on earth,
    Proud man shall never know.

Why wonder that the great and good
    Should kneel, in after-years,
To worship e'en the sacred turf
    That infancy endears;
For o'er the soul emotions crowd
    Tumultuous as the wave;
And shades of dear departed joys
    "Flit shrouded from the grave."

---

\* Author of "The Barber's Shop," "Literary Reminiscences," "Our Turf, our Stage, and our Ring," &c.

I go, loved scene, to distant strife,
    In air impure to pine;
And nevermore these pilgrim feet
    May wander to thy shrine;
Yet memory oft will haunt thy glades,
    Preserve them pure and free,
To bless the little sinless hearts
    That follow after me.

## HOME.

### By Charles Swain.

Home's not merely four square walls,
    Though with pictures hung and gilded;
Home is where affection calls,—
    Fill'd with shrines the heart hath builded!
Home!—go watch the faithful dove,
    Sailing 'neath the heaven above us;
Home is where there's one to love;
    Home is where there's one to love us!

Home's not merely roof and room,—
    It needs something to endear it;
Home is where the heart can bloom,—
    Where there's some kind lip to cheer it!
What is home with none to meet,—
    None to welcome, none to greet us?
Home is sweet—and only sweet—
    When there's one we love to meet us!

## THE MUSIC IN OUR HOME.

(FROM "SONGS OF MY LEISURE HOURS.")

### BY MRS WM. HOBSON.*

'Tis not the harp that fairy fingers
   Sweep, to charm us with its tone,
Although its thrilling echo lingers
   Long and sweetly in our home.

Ah! no; 'tis music that brings brightness
   To the mother's heart and eye,
Telling her that life has flower,
   Lighting up the shadows by.

'Tis the hum of pleasant voices,
   Prattling in sweet childhood's tone,
Making glad the household ingle
   With a music all their own.

'Tis the pattering of light footsteps
   Up and down the homely floor,
With untiring perseverance
   Pacing one path o'er and o'er.

'Tis the merry shout and laughter
   Ringing out in joyous glee,
Making all around re-echo
   With the wild, glad melody.

'Tis the timid first-taught accents
   Of the bonny household pet,
Lisping words to the fond mother
   That she never will forget.

Oh! that home is drear and lonely,
   That has never heard the tone
Of this pleasant fireside music
   From some bright-eyed little one!

---

\* This lady is now Mrs Ferrand, and resides at Ashton-under-Lyne.

## THE SONGS OF OUR FATHERS.

### BY MRS HEMANS.*

> "Sing aloud
> Old songs, the precious music of the heart."
> WORDSWORTH.

SING them upon the sunny hills,
   When days are long and bright,
And the blue gleam of shining rills
   Is loveliest to the sight!
Sing them along the misty moor,
   Where ancient hunters roved;
And swell them through the torrent's roar,
   The songs our fathers loved!

The songs their souls rejoiced to hear
   When harps were in the hall,
And each proud note made lance and spear
   Thrill on the banner'd wall:
The songs that through our valleys green,
   Sent on from age to age,
Like his own river's voice, have been
   The peasant's heritage.

The reaper sings them when the vale
   Is fill'd with plumy sheaves;
The woodman, by the starlight pale,
   Cheer'd homeward through the leaves;
And unto them that glancing oars
   A joyous measure keep,
Where the dark rocks that crest our shores
   Dash back the foaming deep.

So let it be!—a light they shed
   O'er each old font and grove;
A memory of the gentle dead,
   A lingering spell of love.
Murmuring the names of mighty men,
   They bid our streams roll on,
And link high thoughts to every glen
   Where valiant deeds were done.

Teach them your children round the hearth,
    When evening fires burn clear,
And in the fields of harvest mirth,
    And on the hills of deer.
So shall each unforgotten word,
    When far those loved ones roam,
Call back the hearts which once it stirr'd,
    To childhood's holy home.

The green woods of their native land
    Shall whisper in the strain;
The voices of their household band
    Shall breathe their names again;
The heathery heights in vision rise
    Where, like the stag, they roved—
Sing to your sons those melodies,
    The songs your fathers loved.

---

\* Felicia Dorothea Browne was born in Liverpool, on the 25th September 1793. Her mother, whose family name was Wagner, although a German by appellation, was of Italian descent. Her father was a merchant of considerable eminence; but he eventually suffered under those reverses incidental to a commercial life. While his daughter was still very young, he retired with his family into Wales, and resided for some time at Gwrych, near Abergele. While here, a volume of verses by the young poetess, published in 1808, attracted much attention, and was followed within four years by two others. In her nineteenth year, she was married to Captain Hemans, of the 4th Regiment. His health breaking, it became necessary for him, a few years after the marriage, to go to reside in Italy. Mrs Hemans, whose literary pursuits rendered it undesirable for her to leave England, continued to reside with her mother and sister at a quiet and pretty spot near St Asaph, in North Wales, where she commenced the training of her five sons. For their better education, she subsequently (April 1828) fixed her residence at Wavertree, near Liverpool, and still later, (1831,) changed her abode to Dublin. She died on Saturday, the 16th May 1835.

## DOMESTIC MELODY.

(FROM "HOURS WITH THE MUSES.")

### By J. C. Prince.

Though my lot hath been dark for these many long years,
And the cold world hath brought me its trials and fears;
Though the sweet star of hope scarcely looks through the gloom,
And the best of my joys have been quench'd in the tomb;
Yet why should I murmur at Heaven's decree,
While the wife of my home is a solace for me?

Though I toil through the day for precarious food,
With my body worn down, and my spirit subdued:
Though the good things of life seldom enter my door,
And my safety and shelter are far from secure;
Still, still I am rich as a poet may be,
For the wife of my heart is a treasure to me.
Let the libertine sneer, and the cold one complain,
And turn all the purest of pleasures to pain;
There is nothing on earth that can e'er go beyond
A heart that is faithful, and feeling, and fond:
There is but one joy of the highest degree,
And the wife of my soul is that blessing to me.

## HOME AND FRIENDS.

### By Charles Swain.

Oh, there's a *power* to make each hour
　As sweet as heaven design'd it;
Nor need we roam to bring it home,
　Though few there be that find it!
We seek too high for things close by,
　And lose what nature found us;
For 'life hath here no charm so dear
　As Home and Friends around us!

We oft destroy the present joy
　For future hopes—and praise them;
Whilst flowers as sweet bloom at our feet,
　If we'd but stoop and raise them!
For things *afar* still sweetest are,
　When youth's bright spell hath bound us;
But soon we're taught that earth has nought
　Like Home and Friends around us!

The friends that speed in time of need,
　When Hope's last reed is shaken,
To show us still that, come what will,
　We are not quite forsaken:
Though all were night, if but the light
　Of *friendship*'s altar crown'd us,
'Twould prove the bliss of earth was this—
　Our Home and Friends around us!

## MINE!

(A WIFE'S SONG.)

### BY MRS G. LINNÆUS BANKS.

I LOVE thee, I love thee, as dearly as when
    We plighted our troth in the spring-time of life;
The tempests of years have swept o'er us since then,
    Yet affection survives both in Husband and Wife.

No love that the poet e'er fabled of yore
    Could vie in its depth or endurance with mine;
No miser could treasure his glittering store
    As I hoard in my heart every love-tone of thine.

No babe could repose on a fond Mother's breast,
    More calmly confiding than I do on thine;
I fly to thy arms, as a bird to its nest,
    For shelter and safety, dear Husband of mine!

Ay, "Mine, and mine only!" Oh, joy passing words,
    To carol this song in my innermost heart;
"While thine, and thine only!" the vibrating chords
    Shall echo till sense, life, and feeling depart.

---

\* Formerly Miss Isobella Varley, of Manchester, Authoress of "Ivy Leaves,"&c. Mrs Banks has also written a successful novel, entitled "The Manchester Man". Illustrated version £9.95 from PRINTWISE PUBLICATIONS.

---

## THE WOODMAN'S BALLAD.

### BY R. W. PROCTER.

ONE morn, the first of beaming May,
While yet the night-bird tuned her lay,
I wander'd with my youth's first love,
To view the sweets of hill and grove,
And choose wild flowerets, glistening fair,
To wreathe a garland for her hair.

I placed the crown, with heart-felt vow,
Upon her full and radiant brow;
And never did a love-'tranced eye
A rarer May-day queen espy:
I view'd her with unbounded bliss,
My rapture sealing with a kiss.

The blooming lass is now my bride,
The woodman's hope, the woodman's pride;
And crown'd will be my earth-born joys,
If bless'd with smiling girls and boys;
In life's decline a balm to give,
And bid my name and memory live;
E'en when the turf of simple green
Wraps Edwin and his village queen.

## EDITH.
### (FROM "AFTER-BUSINESS JOTTINGS.")

#### BY R. R. BEALEY.

Two years old, and so bonny and fair,
With thy light blue eyes and flaxen hair,
With thy laughing face and chattering tongue,
Thy warm embrace and affection strong;
Thou art indeed as lovely a child
As ever the heart from itself beguiled.

Two years old, like a bud just blown,
Showing the colour and shade alone;
But if, even now, such beauty we see,
What may we hope the full flower to be?
A gem from the hand of the Florist Divine,
In which both the rose and the lily combine.

Oh that thy future may never destroy
That bright merry laugh and innocent joy!
But, pure as the lily, and sweet as the rose,
May thy heart be still fresher as life nears its close.
And at last, when thy summons to leave this earth is given,
May angels transport thee to bloom on in heaven.

## "AS WELCOME AS FLOWERS IN MAY."

(FROM "THE POETIC ROSARY.")

BY J. C. PRINCE.

"As welcome as flowers in May!"
    Kind words with a musical sound;
What can be more welcome than they,
    When fair-footed spring cometh round;
Glad Spring! ever welcome to each,
    To childhood, to manhood, and age,
For she comes to delight us and teach,
    And she opens a beautiful page.

There are many things welcome as these,
    As we thread the dim mazes of life;
A calm sense of pleasure and ease
    After seasons of sorrow and strife—
A feeling of safety and glee
    When a danger, long-threaten'd, is past,
And even the knowledge to see
    That the *worst* has befallen us at last.

Fresh health on the cheek of a child,
    That we fear'd was escaping above;—
A smile from the maid undefiled,
    Who hath kindled one's soul into love;—
The sound of the blithe marriage-bell
    To the bride who has given her heart,
And the words of her husband, that tell
    His devotion will never depart.

The birth of a child, when we feel
    We can foster it, guard it, and guide;
While the smiles of its mother reveal
    Her matchless affection and pride;—
Its first broken syllables, made
    More closely our bosoms to bind,
And its up-growing beauty, display'd
    In the promising dawn of its mind;—

The first pleasant glimpse of our home,
   After travel, with toil and annoy,
When we vow for the moment to roam
   No more from its threshold of joy ;—
Each form more expanded in grace,—
   Each voice more melodious grown ;—
The soul-beaming gladness of face
   Of the whole household treasure our own ;—


Old Ocean's magnificent roar
   To a voyager loving the sea,
And the sight of his dear native shore
   When he cometh back scatheless and free :
The music of brooks and of birds,
   To a captive just loosen'd from thrall,
And the love-lighted looks and sweet words
   Of his wife, who is dearer than all ;—


The soul-touching penitent tears
   Of those who have stray'd from the light,
When they come, with their hopes and their fears,
   To ask us to lead them aright ;—
The frank, cordial look of a foe
   We have conquer'd by kindness and peace,
And the pure satisfaction to know,
   That a friendship begun will increase ;—


And then, in our calm chimney-nook,
   Alone, with a fire burning bright,
How welcome a newly-brought book,
   That has startled the world with delight !
How welcome one's own printed name
   To our first happy efforts in song,
And the first grateful whisper of fame,
   That bids us speed bravely along !


There are many more subjects, no doubt,
   If my muse had but language and time ;
But there's something I must not leave out,
   It will gracefully finish my rhyme :
From a friend how heart-warming to hear
   What his lips with sincerity say,
"Why, your presence brings comfort and cheer ;
   You're as welcome as flowers in May!"

## THE POET TO HIS WIFE.

### By WILLIAM MORT.

I saw thee in the noisy town, a unit 'mid the throng,
Wending thy way, a thing of light, the crowded streets along;
The eyes of men were fix'd upon thy blushing brow and cheek,
As, like a timid fawn, thou pass'd—so beautiful, so meek.

Again, within the sacred dome, I saw thee bent in prayer,—
Oh, well might angels envy man a child so purely fair!
Gracefully as the fuchsia's flower thy gentle head was bow'd,
And sweetly droop'd thine eyes beneath their soft and fringèd shroud.

I know not if 'twere then a sin to have so strange a thought,
But I did look on thee as one from heavenly regions brought;
And though I long'd to touch thy hand, I fear'd the spirit's rod
Might smite me as the man was smote who touch'd the ark of God!

And back I shrunk within myself, like one who had madly striven
To tread with mortal footsteps on the threshold of high heaven:
Upon thy face I gazed again, nor half my danger knew,
Till one sweet glance of thine proclaim'd that *thou* wert mortal too.

And then within thy quiet home I saw thee yet once more,
When smiles as bright as happiness thy cheek were flitting o'er;
When duty, truth, and love engross'd thy every thought and care,
And not a doubt came o'er thy soul to cast a shadow there!

And now thou art my own, beloved, my own most faithful wife,
The silken cord that fetters me to happiness and life.
A gentle tyrant art thou, love, and I hug my chains and thee,—
And who but death shall dare attempt to set the captive free!

---

## THE FIRST-BORN.

### By Mrs Trafford Whitehead.

Sleep, baby, sleep,—and o'er thy infant dreams
   Bend the bright angels, murmuring low and sweet,
Guiding, with shining hands, the soft sunbeams
   Upon thy future,—and beneath thy feet
Holding the shadows that would upward creep.
Calm be the peace around!—sleep, baby, sleep!

What hath the future 'neath those dreaming eyes?
   Childhood's light joys, and babbling griefs and fears,
And youth's bewildering thoughts, deep, wild, and wise,
   Bright flitting summer clouds that break in tears,
And manhood's whirling night-mists, hurrying past;
The stormy wind, guiding to port at last.

Hath Time some secret to disclose to thee,
   Thou with the tiny hands, that to the world
Shall bring new light, making the darkness flee?
   Perchance the cloak of ignorance to chaos hurl'd.
Hath life some mystery that thou shalt live to reap,
That God hath saved for thee? Sleep, baby, sleep!

How faint thy wailing cry, that loud and shrill
   May wake the echoes from the vales of gloom,
Where ignorance hovers,—mind and power of will
   Do fling a radiance of immortal doom!
Weak be thy waving arms,—yet in their circling hold
Shall mortals limit truths God hath not told.

We know the future hath a glorious store,
   We know that life is vast and serious;
And those that fate hath bless'd are known before,
   And weave materials imperious.
The weakest grasp may give the grandest gift,—
The tardiest step may far outrace the swift.

And who shall say that, in their counsels low,
   The murmuring angels may not yet unseal
Some mystery the world doth pant to know,
   Those infant lips are chosen to reveal?
The thread that shall unroll truth's gordian coil
Perchance lies in those hands' allotted toil.

I would not ask that glory's clarion peal
   Should sound thy name loud through the wander-
     ing earth;
But that its accents human hearts should feel,
   When high was meeded honour, lauded worth;
Where'er the great and good, the pure and free
Are found,—there in the shining midst, would I seek
   thee!

## THE STAR OF THE HOUSEHOLD.

### By John Critchley Prince.

An angel in the house? Ah, yes!
   There is a precious angel there;
A woman, form'd to soothe and bless,
   Good, if she be not fair;
A kindly, patient, faithful wife,
   Cheerful, and of a temper mild,
One who can lend new charms to life,
   And make man reconciled.

Oh! 'tis a pleasant thing to see
    Such being going to and fro,
With aspect genial and free,
    Yet pure as spotless snow:
One who performs her duties, too,
    With steady and becoming grace,
Giving to each attention due,
    In fitting time and place.

One who can use her husband's means
    With careful thrift from day to day,
And when misfortune intervenes
    Put needless wants away;
Who smooths the wrinkles from his brow,
    When more than common cares oppress;
And cheers him—faithful to her vow—
    With hopeful tenderness.

One who, when sorrow comes, can feel
    With woman's tenderness of heart;
And yet can strive with quiet zeal
    To ease another's smart;
One who, when fortune's sun grows bright,
    And flings the clouds of care aside,
Can bask with pleasure in its light,
    Yet feel no foolish pride.

One who can check, with saint-like power,
    Wild thoughts that spring to dangerous birth,
And wake pure feelings, as the shower
    Of spring awakes the earth;
Bring forth the latent virtues shrined
    Within the compass of the breast,
And to the weak and tortured mind
    Give confidence and rest.

Good neighbour—not to envy prone;
    True wife, in luxury or need;
Fond mother, not unwisely shown;
    Blameless in thought and deed:
Whoever claims so rare a wife,
    Thus should his earnest words be given—
" She is the angel of my life,
    And makes my home a heaven!"

## " 'TIS SWEET TO MEET THE FRIEND WE LOVE."

### By George Richardson.

'Tis sweet to meet the friend we love,
   By distance kept apart for years;
And dearer when such joys are link'd
   To those which kindred more endears.

Give me the still, domestic home—
   The humble hearth, the lowly state—
Contentment, and inspiring peace—
   Life's chiefest blessings to await.

The welcome fare, the cheerful smile,
   The tree-embower'd cot of thatch;
My gentle wife and offspring dear,
   With none but friend to raise my latch.

These are the chiefest worldly gifts,
   Sweet joys which final blessings prove;
And what is life, unless to live
   In social intercourse and love?

I ask not honour, crave not wealth,
   But just enough of fortune's smile
To check adversity and want,
   By honest means and moderate toil.

With these to move in decent pride,
   Through varied scenes this chequer'd maze—
To love and live endear'd to mine,
   And pass in peacefulness my days!

## WELCOME, BONNY BRID!

### By Samuel Laycock.

Tha 'rt welcome, little bonny brid,
But shouldn't ha' come just when tha did;
      Toimes are bad.
We're short o' pobbies for eawr Joe,
But that, of course, tha didn't know,
      Did ta, lad?

Aw 've often yeard mi feyther tell,
'At when aw coom i' th' world misel
      Trade wur slack;
An' neaw it's hard wark pooin' throo—
But aw munno fear thee; iv aw do
      Tha 'll go back.

Cheer up! these toimes 'ull awter soon;
Aw 'm beawn to beigh another spoon—
      One for thee;
An' as tha's sich a pratty face,
Aw 'll let thee have eawr Charley's place
      On mi knee.

God bless thee, love, aw 'm fain tha 'rt come,
Just try an' mak thisel awhoam:
      What ar 't co'd?
Tha 'rt loike thi mother to a tee,
But tha's thi feyther's nose, aw see,
      Well, aw 'm blow'd!

Come, come, tha needn't look so shy,
Aw am no' blackin' thee, not I;
      Settle deawn,
An' tak this haup'ney for thisel',
There's lots o' sugar-sticks to sell
      Deawn i' th' teawn.

Aw know when furst aw coom to th' leet
Aw're fond o' owt 'at tasted sweet;
      Tha'll be th' same.
But come, tha's never towd thi dad
What he's to co thi yet, mi lad—
      What's thi name?

Hush! hush! tha munno cry this way,
But get this sope o' cinder tay
      While it's warm;
Mi mother used to give it me,
When aw wur sich a lad as thee,
      In her arm.

Hush a babby, hush a bee—
Oh, what a temper! dear a-me
      Heaw tha skroikes:
Here's a bit o' sugar, sithee;
Howd thi noise, an' then aw'll gie thee
      Owt tha loikes.

We'n nobbut getten coarsish fare,
But eawt o' this tha'st ha' thi share,
      Never fear.
Aw hope tha'll never want a meel,
But allus fill thi bally weel
      While tha'rt here.

Thi feyther's noan bin wed so long,
An' yet tha sees he's middlin' throng
      Wi' yo' o:
Besides thi little brother, Ted,
We'n one up-steers, asleep i' bed
      Wi' eawr Joe.

But though we'n childer two or three,
We'll mak' a bit o' reawm for thee—
      Bless thee, lad!
Tha'rt th' prattiest brid we han i' th' nest;
Come, hutch up closer to mi breast—
      Aw'm thi dad.

## THE LOST BROTHER.

### By William Mort.

Mother, look forth on yon beautiful cloud,
   That sails o'er the bright blue sky,
And flings to the winds its misty shroud
   As it maketh its course on high;
And tell me if that is my brother, who's gone
   To those dwellings of light above,
Where the sun in his glory for ever hath shone?
   —That is *not* thy brother, my love!

Look, mother, look at yon twinkling star,
   That glows like a light on the sea,
And seemeth as though from its palace afar
   It were steadfastly gazing on me.
Is not *that* my brother who fled away
   From his home like a wild stock-dove,
And left me all alone to play?
   —That is *not* thy brother, my love!

List, mother, list to the soft low tone
   That comes on the evening breeze,
Like the musical sounds some night-birds moan
   As it steals through the old elm-trees;
Is not *that* the voice of my brother, who's telling
   The joys of his home above—
Where the throat of archangel with rapture is
      swelling?
   —That is *not* thy brother, my love!

The clouds that flit o'er the sky so bright,
   Soon, soon have pass'd away;
And the star that cheereth the gloom of night
   Is gone ere the break of day.
But thy brother—oh think not, my love, that he
   Doth change like the things of air!
The heaven of heavens no eye can see—
   Thy brother, thy brother is *there!*

## EVENING SONG.

(FROM "HOURS WITH THE MUSES.")

### BY J. C. PRINCE.

'TIS wearing late! 'tis wearing late! I hear the vesper bell!
And o'er yon misty hill the sun hath look'd a bright farewell;
The bee is in its honey-home, the bird is in its nest,
And every living being yearns for solace and for rest;
The household gathers round the hearth, and loving souls draw near,—
Young mothers, rock, young mothers, rock, oh, rock your children dear.

It is the hour, the happy hour, when I was wont to be
Hush'd to a calm and blessèd sleep upon my mother's knee;
While she would sing, with voice subdued, and ever-tuneful tongue,
Some well-remember'd melody, some old and simple song;
And sometimes on my cheek would fall affection's holy tear,—
Young mothers, rock, young mothers, rock, oh, rock your children dear.

It is the heart-awakening time, when breezes rock the rose,
Which drooping folds its vernal leaves in nature's soft repose;
And silvery-wingèd butterflies, in field or garden fair,
Are swinging in their dewy beds by every passing air;
And birds are rock'd in cradles green, till morning's hues appear,—
Young mothers, rock, young mothers, rock, oh, rock your children dear.

The starry-girdled moon looks down, and sees her welcome beam
Rock'd on the undulating breast of ocean, lake, and stream;
And mariners, who love her light, are rock'd by wave and wind,
Pining for home, and all its joys, which they have left behind,
Till Hope's sweet sunshine comes again, their sickening souls to cheer,—
Young mothers, rock, young mothers, rock, oh, rock your children dear.

Oh! it would be a pleasant thing, had we the will and power,
To change the present for the past, and fly to childhood's hour;
To seek old haunts, to hear old tales, resume our former play;
To live in joyous innocence but one, *one* little day,
Oh! that would be a precious pause on life's unknown career.—
Young mothers, rock, young mothers, rock, oh, rock your children dear.

## LOVED AND LOST.

### By Mrs Trafford Whitehead.

The grave hath won thee, and thy happy home
  Shall know thy place no more! Where thou didst roam,
Amongst thy shrubs and flowers, thy feet shall glide
With lingering steps no more! The world is wide—
Why hath Death taken *thee?* when every hour
Some weary one, with failing strength, doth cower
'Neath the delaying grasp. Why doth his decree
Fix with relentless hold, thou well-beloved, on *thee?*

Death! stand thou back. Is this the victim, bound
In thy cold, stony grasp? Is there no breath
On those red lips? Do I not hear a sound?
Will she not speak again? O Death! O Death!
Arouse thee! I am pressing thy still hand:
Thou dost but linger near the spirit-land.
Can we not wake thee? Thou art silent—*thou*—
Can there be death for me on that bright brow?

How I have kiss'd that calm and icy cheek,
For all it wears a cold, repellant guise!
Thy nature was so loving and so meek,
I seek in vain some message from those eyes.
Why art thou here at mid-day, hush'd and still,
With the light closed on thee? Thy words do thrill
Through the long passages, as last they fell,
And thou art lying here. Is this Farewell?
Why do we stand around thy silent bed
Unwelcomed and unheeded? Thou art dead!

The slow, dull rain is dripping dully on;
With a soft, grieving sound;—the wind wails on,
As though it mourn'd thee lying stilly here;
Thou—the spirit of the place—to all so dear.
How beautiful thou art with that faint smile!
How fair thy lilied cheek! how calm thine eyes,
Closed in a placid sleep of peace the while
That we are bow'd with grief—thou pure! thou wise!
God sent His messenger across the sky,

Through the night-stricken world, so tenderly.
He found thee panting with thy weary breath,
And seal'd the smile upon thy lips—in death.

How the long dreary months will come and go,
Making the grass grow longer on thy grave!
And some shall bring it leaves, and some but snow,
And the sad winds shall o'er it moan and wave;
Yet thou wilt still be voiceless in the time,
When coming years shall ring forth other chime.
Voiceless! not so; a voice is left for thee—
The boy, the child of thine idolatry—
And thou be voiceless while he lives to speak
Thy thoughts, thy words, in accents faint and weak,
But still thine own. Thou hast a future cast
In thy fair child; not to the hurried past,
Snapp'd so abruptly, is thy lot confined:
Destiny, striking, pities—Fate is kind.

And when in after-years, a child no more,
He stands beside thy grave with bowèd head,
Will he remember times that now are o'er?
Will he remember thee, who now art dead?
Will thy pale cheek, thy soft and tender eyes
Upon the mirror of his mind arise?
Will the dark gloss of that luxuriant hair
Bring back the gentle face, so kind and fair?
Smiling upon him in his childish glee,
Blending thy image with his infancy.

The grave hath won thee, let it well take care;
Thou art but lent unto its keeping, like a gem
Too precious for the world to fret and wear,
Befitting rather Heaven's diadem.
Take thy calm rest, beyond all earthly guile,
Deepening upon thy face that moonlight smile.
Ah! thou hast pass'd the gates; we drooping stand,
Watching the vistas of the spirit-land;
And thou canst aid us not, canst give no signs
To her who loved thee, and who wrote these lines.

# EAWR BESSY.

(FROM "AFTER-BUSINESS JOTTINGS.")

By RICHARD R. BEALEY.

Eawr Bessy's gone to th' Sunday schoo',
   What does t'a think o' that?
Hoo wesh'd her face, and comm'd her yure,
   An' donn'd her Sunday hat;
An' then hoo said, 'twur toime to goo—
   Aw couldn't get her t' stay;
Hoo said hoo wish'd 'ut Sunday schoo'
   Wur comin' every day.

For everythin' hoo loikes so weel,
   An' th' teychers are so koind,
Hoo couldn't think to stop awhoam,
   Nor be a bit behoind.
Bu' then hoo allus wur so good,
   An' not a bit loike th' rest;
Aw think hoo's loike those childer 'd be,
   'Ut th' Saviour took an' bless'd.

But summat in her pratty face
   Seems t' say hoo isn't strung,
An' oft aw've thought hoo wur too good
   T' be eawt o' heaven lung;
An' mony a toime at neet aw've dreamt
   'Ut hoo wur ta'en away
Bi th' angels, an' aw've wakken'd up,
   An' fretted o that day.

Aw couldno' help it, 'twur no use
   Heawever aw met try;
An' every neaw an' then hoo'd ax
   What made her mammy cry;
An' then hoo'd kiss me, th' little thing,
   An' sattle on my knee,
An' cuddle me, an' ax me t' sing,
   Or else hoo'd sing for me.

An' so hoo dried up th' sheawers o' rain,
   An' melted th' frost an' snow,
An' brought back summer toime again,
   An' made th' sweet fleawers to grow;
Aw wur so happy at thoose toimes,
   My heart were full o' glee,
We 'd such a lot o' happiness,
   Had little Bess an' me.


Aw recollect, one afternoon,
   When hoo wur sittin' still,
An' readin' in hur little book,
   Bu' favvor'd bein' ill—
Aw stood an' watch'd her for a bit,
   An' wonder'd while aw stood,
If onythin' i' heaven above
   Wur 's bonny an' as good.


Her yure wur just loike threads o' gowd,
   Or curlin' rays o' th' sun,
'Ut hung abeawt her little neck,
   As not o' purpose done;
Bu' theer they lay, as if they'd fo'n
   Just loike to th' flakes o' snow,
So gently, 'ut they seem'd afeard
   To let eawr Bessy know.


Her e'en wur loike to th' summer sky,
   For bein' clear and blue;
An' then her cheeks were loike a rose,
   'Ut th' red wur peepin' through.
An' if yo con but understond,
   Her face, it seem'd to me,
Wur loike a tune upon a harp—
   A moulded melody.


An' as hoo sat, an' as hoo look'd,
   Aw winnot try to tell,
Heaw happy an' heaw fear'd aw wur,
   Nor heaw my breast did swell.
Aw couldn't tell it if aw would,
   But if aw could, thae sees,
Aw 'd rayther keep it to mysel',
   For thee it metna please.

Well, as aw stood a-lookin' so,
   An' watchin' her on th' sly,
Aw seed a tear fo on her book,
   An' loike a diamond lie.
An' then hoo sobb'd as if her heart
   Wur gooin' t' brast i' two,
An' th' tears fell loike a summer sheawer,
   As if they'd weet her through.

For th' little angel, as hoo is,
   Wur readin', as aw fun',
O' Joseph's nowty brethren,
   An' th' mischief as they'd done;
'Twas when hoo'd getten just to th' place
   Where Joseph's sowd away
To th' Ishmaelites, hoo brasted eawt,
   An' begg'd 'em t' let him stay.

Ay, ay, it wur a bonny seet
   As e'er a mortal seed;
An' of a bonnier, why aw'm sure,
   'Ut th' angels ha' no need.
Aw did thank God he'd g'en me th' lass,
   An' couldna' help bu' pray,
'Ut if it wur His blessed will,
   He'd let her wi' me stay.

But here hoo comes, God bless her heart,
   Hoo's bin to th' Sunday schoo',
An' looks as breet as summer-toime,
   An' beawt a shadow, too.
Hoo's getten summat in her yed
   To tell me, aw con see;
An' hoo'll be readin' it to-neet,
   Wi' th' book set on my knee.

An' when hoo says her prayers, aw know
   Hoo'll say, " God bless my dad,
An' dunno' let him drink again—
   It ma'es him swear so bad;
An' God bless mammy, an' eawr Bill;
   And bless eawr Sally too;"
An' then hoo'll goo to bed an' sleep,
   As nobbut good folk do.

# THE CHILD AND THE DEWDROPS.

## IN MEMORY OF A LOST SON.

### BY J. C. PRINCE.

" O DEAREST mother! tell me, pray,
   Why are the dewdrops gone so soon?
Could they not stay till close of day,
To sparkle on the flowery spray,
   Or on the fields till noon?"

The mother gazed upon her boy,
   Earnest with thought beyond his years,
And felt a sharp and sad annoy,
That meddled with her deepest joy;
   But she restrain'd her tears.

" My child, 'tis said such beauteous things,
   Too often loved with vain excess,
Are swept away by angel wings,
Before contamination clings
   To their frail loveliness.
" Behold yon rainbow, brightening yet,
   To which all mingled hues are given!
These are thy dewdrops, grandly set
In a resplendent coronet
   Upon the brow of heaven!

" No stain of earth can reach them there:
   Woven with sunbeams there they shine,
A transient vision of the air,
But yet a symbol, pure and fair,
   Of love and peace divine!"

The boy gazed upward into space,
   With eager and inquiring eyes,
While o'er his fair and thoughtful face
Came a faint glory, and a grace
   Transmitted from the skies.

Ere the last odorous sigh of May,
   That child lay down beneath the sod;
Like dew his young soul pass'd away,
To mingle with the brighter ray
   That veils the throne of God.

Mother! thy fond, foreboding heart
   Truly foretold thy loss and pain;
But thou didst choose the patient part
Of resignation to the smart,
   And own'd thy loss his gain.

## TO LITTLE ANGEL "CHARLIE."

(FROM "AFTER-BUSINESS JOTTINGS.")

BY R. R. BEALEY.

OFTEN have I been to see thee,
   And, while waiting at the door,
I have heard thy small feet patter,
   Patter, on the lobby floor:
     No, I ne'er shall hear thee more.

Then I've greeted thee with kisses,
   Each one loving to the core;
And thy laugh has been like sunshine
   From the bright and heavenly shore:
     But I must not hear thee more.

Ere thy tongue had learn'd to prattle,
   Thoughts were in thee quite a store,
And thine eyes were telling stories,
   All of Love's rich golden lore;
     Yet I may not hear thee more.

As an infant I address'd thee,
   Yea, thy love I did implore;
And I question'd thee in earnest
   Of thy life in days of yore,
     As I may not ask thee more.

Yet I cannot think thee absent,
   But as near me as before;
Or at most, that thou hast shifted
   To the other side the door—
     Lost to sight, and nothing more.

May I not in spirit meet thee,
   When the night is coming o'er?
May I not in shadows greet thee,
   While the breezes softly pour
      Tones of thine from yonder shore?

May I not in dreamland see thee
   Smiling as in days of yore?
Only fairer, and more lovely;
   And although I mayn't adore,
      I still will love thee more and more.

Yes! for death is not a parting,
   Only darkness coming o'er;
Soon our eyes shall all be open'd,
   When the truth we will explore,
      With our loved ones evermore.

Teach me, little angel "Charlie,"
   Teach my spirit, I implore,
Nearer truth! oh, gather garlands,
   Fling them back on earth's dark shore,
      And I will learn as ne'er before.

## THE LAST BEHEST.

### By William Mort.

> "The tongues of dying men
> Enforce attention, like deep harmony."
> Shakspere.

Come hither, wife! I'd speak with thee a while before
    I go,
Once more I'd commune with thee ere I yield me to
    the blow;
Long,.long we've lived together since thy maiden
    heart I won—
Come hither, I would speak with thee ere yet my
    course is run!

Oh, well hast thou perform'd the vows upon the altar
    made,
And kindly tended me when God afflictions on me
    laid;
Ay, truly hast thou cherish'd me, my own, my faith-
    ful wife—
Come hither, I would speak with thee ere yet I part
    with life!

My sons, too, and my darling girl—my Kate—oh, bring
    them all,
And let me gaze upon you till in death's cold arms I
    fall;—
My little ones! nay, do not mourn—I leave your
    mother here;
And God who cheers the widow's heart will dry the
    orphan's tear!

My son, my oldest one, approach,—to thee my charge
    is great,
For thou alone of all my flock hast wrought to man's
    estate;
Oh, look thou on my children with a brother's watch-
    ful eye,
And lead them up in holiness—oh, promise, ere I die!

Thy sister, too—remember, son, thou art her father
 *now;*
Protect her, that no bitter thought may cloud her
 maiden brow;
Guard thou her name with jealousy—each sorrow
 strive to quell—
Cling to her with a brother's love—oh, shield thy sister
 well!

But most, oh, most, my son, support thy mother's fail-
 ing years—
Her heart is stricken by the blast, her eyes are "founts
 of tears;"
I leave her to thee as a gem more rich, more dear
 than life—
My only solace upon earth—my own, my faithful wife!

Oft hath she watch'd thy restless couch when toss'd
 by infant woe;
Oft hath her bosom throbb'd for thee, ere thou her
 cares could know;
And now—look on her, son—she needs that anxious
 care repaid—
Oh, be thou her support when I in the cold grave am
 laid!

Come hither—closer—all of you—I feel that death is
 nigh;
Come closer—closer still—now kiss my cheek before
 I die!
Bless you, my children! bless you all! through life,
 in joy or woe!
A father's blessing be with you!—all—all he can be-
 stow!

## "GOD BLESS THESE POOR WIMMEN THAT'S CHILDER!"

### By Thomas Brierley.

God bless these poor wimmen that's childer!
    Shuz [choose] whether they're rich or they're poor,
Thur's nob'dy con tell whot a woman
    Wi' little uns has to endure;
The times that hoo's wakken i' th' neet-time,
    Attendin' thur wailin and pain,
Un' smoothin' thur pillow of sickness,
    Would crack ony patient mon's brain.

God bless these poor wimmen that's childer!
    Heaw patient they are i' distress!
An infant that God has afflicted
    Does ever a woman love less?
Not hur! The sick creatur hoo watches,
    Wi' caution ten-fowd in hur ee,
Hoo'll never lose seet on't a minute,
    For fear it should happen to dee.

God bless these poor wimmen that's childer!
    Aw deem it a very fine treat
To sit eawt o' seet, un' be watchin'
    A woman gi' th' childer some meat;
Heaw pleasant un' smilin' hur nature,
    Hur face is surrounded wi' joy,
Hoo's dealing o th' childer a fist full,
    Un' plenty on table t' put by.

God bless these poor wimmen that's childer!
    Aw know that they'n mony a fort [fault,]
But chaps has no 'kashun to chuckle,
    Men's blemishes are not so short:
Then have a kind word for these wimmen,
    If t' maddest un' vilest o' men
Wurn just made i' wimmen a fortneet,
    They'd never beat wimmen agen.

God bless these poor wimmen that's childer!
    These smoothers of sorrow and death,
These angels of softness and mercy,
    That comfort as long as they've breath;
These magical charmers of manhood,
    These wreathers of love and delight,
These fairies that never desert us,
    God bless 'um, aw say, wi' yo'r might!

---

## THE KISS BENEATH THE HOLLY.

(FROM "SONGS OF MY LEISURE HOURS.")

### BY MRS WILLIAM HOBSON.

"BE merry and wise," says the good old song,
    And joy to the heart that penn'd it;
If we've aught to fret, the stately "pet"
    Will never reform or mend it.
On Christmas night, when the log burns bright,
    To be joyous is not folly;
There's nought amiss in the playful kiss
    That's stolen beneath the holly.

Let hand clasp hand with a hearty clasp,
    To all give a welcome greeting;
Fling pride afar; don't gloom or mar
    The coming Christmas meeting.
"Be merry and wise," say sparkling eyes,
    Away with all melancholy—
There's nought amiss, just laugh at the kiss
    That's stolen beneath the holly.

Oh, welcome with glee the festive night,
    When the joyous bells are ringing;
But once a year the chime we hear,
    That the Christmas time is bringing.
Don't pout or frown 'neath the mystic crown—
    To be joyous is not folly;
There's nought amiss in the Christmas kiss
    That's stolen beneath the holly.

## MI GRONFEYTHER.

### By Samuel Laycock.

Aw 've just bin a havin' a peep at th' farm-heawse
   Wheer mi gronfeyther lived at so long;
So aw'll draw eawt a bit ov a sketch o' th' owd spot,
   An' work it up into a song.
An' furst let me tell yo' aw'm sorry to foind
   'At th' place isn't same as it wur;
For th' di'mond-shaped windows han o bin pood eawt,
   An' they'n ta'en th' wooden latch off o' th' dur.

They'n shifted that seeat wheer mi gronfeyther sat
   Ov a neet when he'rn readin' th' Owd Book.
An' aw couldn't foind th' nail wheer he hung up his hat,
   Though aw bother'd an' seech'd for 't i' th' nook.
There's th' dog-kennel yonder, an' th' hencote aw see,
   An' th' clooas-prop just stonds as it did;
There's a brid-cage hangs up wheer mi gronfeyther's wur,
   But aw couldn't see owt ov a brid.

When aw wur a lad abeawt thirteen, or so,
   Aw remember aw'd mony a good ride;
For mi gronfeyther 'd getten a horse or two then,
   An' a noice little jackass beside.
An' then he'd a garden at th' backside o' th' heawse
   Wheer eawr Bobby an' me used to ceawer,
Eatin' goosbris, an' currans, an' ruburb, an' crabs,
   Or owt there wur else 'at wur seawer.

Mi gronfeyther—bless him—reet doated o' me—
   He'd tell me aw geet a foine lad;
An' mony a toime say, when aw'rn sit on his knee,
   "Eh, bless thee; tha favvers thi dad!"

A rare foine owd fellow mi gronfeyther wur,
   Wi' a regular big Roman nose;
An' though nearly eighty, he look'd strong an' hale,
   An' his cheeks wur'n as red as a rose.
There wur nowt abeawt him 'at wur shabby or mean;
   An' he wur no' beawt brains in his skull:
He wur allus streightforrud i' o 'at he did—
   An owd-fashun'd Yorkshur John Bull.

He'd a farm ov his own, an' a noice little pond,
   Wheer we used to go fishin' for treawt;
An' aw haven't forgetten when th' hay time coom reawnd,
   For us childer had mony a blow eawt.
An' when th' "heawsin" wur done, eh, we had some rare fun,
   Wi' tipplin' an' rowlin' on th' stack;
An' then mi owd gronfeyther 'd come wi' his pipe,
   An' we o used to climb on his back.
Then he'd tell mi aunt Betty to beigh me some spice;
   An' whenever hoo happen'd to bake,
He'd tell her to reach deawn a pot o' presarves,
   An' mak' me a noice presarve cake.

God bless him, he's gone; an' a kinder owd mon
   Never walk'd o' two legs nor he wur;
Th' last time aw wur o'er theer, an' seed him alive,
   He coom back wi' me ever so fur.
Aw geet howd ov his hont when we parted that neet,
   An aw think aw shall never forget
Heaw he look'd i' mi face when he'rn goin' away:
   It wur th' last time 'at ever we met.

A week or two after, th' owd fellow 'd a stroke,—
   He fell off his cheer on to th' floor;
They gether'd him up, an' they took him to bed,
   But he never wur gradely no moor.
Good-bye, dear owd gronfeyther; nob'dy, aw know,
   Could be fonder nor aw wur o' thee;
Aw shall never forget heaw tha patted mi yed,
   When aw used to be ceawr'd on thi knee.

## LINES TO MY WIFE

DURING HER RECOVERY FROM A LONG ILLNESS.

### By Samuel Bamford.

The youthful bard doth chant his lay
    To nymph or goddess fair;
The thirsty bard doth Bacchus pray
    For wine to drown his care;
And some have sung of olden time,
    And feats of chivalry;
And shall not I address a rhyme,
    My own dear wife, to thee?

Full thirty years have o'er us pass'd
    Since thou and I were wed,
And time hath dealt us many a blast,
    And somewhat bow'd thine head,
And torn thine hair, thy bright brown hair,
    That stream'd so wild and free;
But oh! thy tresses still are fair
    And beautiful to me!

Yes, Time hath ta'en thy lily hand,
    And chill'd thy stream of life;
And scored some channels with his wand,
    As envying thee, my wife:
But let not sorrow make thee sigh,
    Nor care thy heart distress;
Though health do fail, and charms do fly,
    Thy husband will thee bless!

Ay! bless thy cheek, all worn and wan,
    With beauty once beset;
The red rose leaves, my love, are gone;
    The pale ones linger yet:
And bless thy care-beclouded brow,
    And bless thy dimmèd sight;
Can I forget the time when thou
    Wert my young morning-light?

We ranged the bowers, we cull'd the flowers,
   By upland and by dell;
And many a night, by pale moonlight,
   We sought the lonely well.
And many a night, when all above
   Shone not one starlit ray;
And was not I thy Wizard, love?
   And wert thou not my Fay?


One arm was o'er thy shoulder cast;
   One hand was held in thine;
Whilst thy dear arm my youthful waist
   Did trustfully entwine:
And through the night, all still and stark,
   No other footsteps near,
We stray'd; and, love, it was not dark,—
   My light of life was there!


Oh, light of love! oh, early born!
   Love-born and lost too soon!
Oh, love! we often thought it morn,
   When it was early noon!
And, love! we thought it still was noon,
   When eve came o'er the land;
And, love! we deem'd it wondrous soon
   When midnight was at hand.


And when at length we needs must part,
   And could no longer stay;
Still hand in hand, and heart by heart,
   We homewards took our way:
The wild-flowers laved our ling'ring feet,
   The woodbine shed its dew;
And o'er the meads and pastures sweet
   The night-wind freely blew.


The rubies from thy lips may fade,
   Thy cheek be pale and cold;
But thou wert mine, a youthful maid,
   And I'll be thine when old!
I see those tears that grateful start,
   Oh! turn them not aside;
But, dear one! come unto my heart,
   As when thou wert my bride.

## ANGEL ANNIE.

### By Mrs William Hobson.

She came, a little fairy one,
   And nestled to my breast;
Came, as a truant dove would turn,
   And seek its parent nest;
Her soft blue eye beam'd with a light
   That was not caught from earth;
Her coral lips smiled with a love
   That had an angel's birth.

She grew; grew with the summer flowers—
   A little violet wild,
A rosebud with immortal soul—
   A lovely, winning child.
The stranger e'en would hush his breath
   To hear her soft, low tone;
'Twas like the echo of some harp,
   Heard but in heaven alone.

'Twas strange how close the little one
   Was wreathed about my heart;
She was amongst the things from which
   My memory could not part.
I never see the violet bloom,
   The little daisy peep,
But I think of her, the " gather'd flower "—
   I think of her and weep.

Death came, and found upon her face
   Strange, wondrous beauty there;
A light shone round her baby brow,
   And rippled in her hair;
She turn'd and said, with heavenly smile,
   Bright, yet foreboding sorrow,
" Mamma, I shall not want my curls—
   Not want my curls to-morrow."

And then her blue eyes quivering closed,
    She softly went to sleep ;
The little bird had flutter'd home—
    It seem'd a sin to weep :
A sin to weep! yet, oh, to stand
    Beside that darling one,
And feel the starry light of home
    Had with her spirit gone !

We knew the prattling voice was hush'd,
    The lisping, love-taught word
Would ne'er again call forth a joy,
    Would ne'er again be heard ;
The pattering step, the little hand
    That lovingly sought ours,
Would never more be clasp'd by us,
    Nor seek the summer flowers.

We knew that God had care of her,
    The peerless angel one,
And that no wintry wind would blight
    The flowers where she had gone.
But oh! 'twas grief, deep grief, to watch
    Beside the little bed—
To gaze upon the household pet,
    And know that she was dead !

## MY IDEAL HOME.

### By Mrs William Hobson.

"A thing of beauty is a joy for ever."—Keats.

Nor in the city, nor the crowded town,
   Where the faint breeze with fever's ever rife;
Not where those heated hives look darkly down
   Upon the hum of ever-warring strife;
Nor 'midst the classic shrines of that fair land
   Whose fame is sung in ancient poets' story,
Though the blue Ægean waves roll o'er her strand,
   And sculptured ruins give their hallow'd glory.

Give me a homestead in an English vale;
   A little, sunny, and secluded spot,
Where the sweet dove and minstrel nightingale
   Would chime their vespers round my lowly cot;
Where the soft, balmy breeze of summer comes,
   Laden with perfume from the violet wild:
Where the forget-me-not its blue eye suns—
   Fair summer's lowliest, yet most lovely child.

I'd have it nestling near thick-foliaged trees;
   The rippling stream should tell its harp-notes near,
And mingle with the sighing of the breeze,
   Charming with music the enraptured ear;
A river, winding like a silver thread,
   Should roll its ever-dancing waves along,
And spangling o'er its sinuous, mossy bed,
   The fairest flowers breathe their voiceless song.

The gushing grape should hang its trailing vine,
   The tinted apple and the juicy pear
With silvery blossoms in the summer shine,
   And autumn find their golden fruitage there;
The blushing rose, with dewy, drooping head,
   Should twine around the window of my room,
Like some fair Cupid, with love's wings outspread,
   Whisp'ring sweet stories of the gorgeous June.

I would not have a grand and lordly home,
  Where the famed artist had spent all his skill
To decorate and carve each fretted dome,
  The gazer's mind with wonderment to fill;
The only gilding should be nature's green,
  Her living tracery of flowers and leaves;
A little gem set in an emerald scene,
  With fond, true hearts beneath its peaceful eaves.

Within the room fair jewels from afar,
  Wrought on the canvas, breathing full of life,
Should whisper to us, like a lone, bright star,
  Of ages past, of minds with beauty rife;
The chisell'd form, cut from the tinted stone,
  The sighing shell, the flowerets of the sea,
Rare gems of art, from climes beyond our own,
  Cluster'd around, in fairy groups should be.

I'd have the antique book with gleanings old,
  The master-minds of every land and age;
Deep science, with her wealth of sterling gold,
  Scatter'd like pearls upon the mystic page;
The poet's lyre—the soul-wrought, breathing lyre,
  Immortal Shakespeare, and the laurel'd throng,
With glowing imagery, and thoughts of fire,
  Should wile the dreamy twilight hours along.

The broken-hearted and the weary one,
  The orphan, friendless, and the homeless poor,
Should ne'er in vain with sorrow's story come—
  A ready hand would freely give its store;
True love within each heart and word should live,
  The deep, devoted love, that knows no bliss
Beyond the feeling that its well-springs give—
  Who would not gladly claim a home like this?

## IV.

### Songs of Life and Brotherhood.

#### THE SONGS OF THE PEOPLE.

AN ORIGINAL SONG, WRITTEN EXPRESSLY FOR THIS VOLUME.

By John Critchley Prince.

Oh! the songs of the people are voices of power,
    That echo in many a land;
They lighten the heart in the sorrowful hour,
    And quicken the labour of hand;
They gladden the shepherd on mountain and plain,
    And the sailor who travels the sea;
The poets have chanted us many a strain,
    But the songs of the people for me.

The artisan, wandering forth early to toil,
    Sings a snatch of old song by the way;
The ploughman, who sturdily furrows the soil,
    Meets the breeze with the words of his lay:
The man at the stithy, the maid at her wheel,
    The mother with babe at her knee,
Oft utter some simple old rhymes, which they feel—
    Oh! the songs of the people for me.

An anthem of triumph, a ditty of love,
    A carol 'gainst sorrow and care,
A hymn of the household, soft, rising above
    The music of hope or despair;
A song patriotic, how grand is the sound
    To all who desire to be free!
A song of the heart, how it makes others bound!—
    Oh! the songs of the people for me.

## "WHY, PRITHEE NOW."

### By John Byrom, M.A., F.R.S.

Why, prithee now, what does it signify,
   For to bustle and make such a rout?
It is virtue alone that can dignify,
   Whether clothèd in ermine or clout.
Come, come, and maintain thy discretion;
   Let it act a more generous part;
For I find, by thy honest confession,
   That the world has too much of thy heart.

Beware that its fatal ascendancy
   Do not tempt thee to mope and repine;
With a humble and hopeful dependency
   Still await the good pleasure divine.
Success in a higher beatitude
   Is the end of what's under the pole;
A philosopher takes it with gratitude,
   And believes it is best on the whole.

The world is a scene, thou art sensible,
   Upon which, if we do but our best,
On a wisdom that's incomprehensible,
   We may safely rely for the rest.
Then trust to its kind distribution,
   And, however things happen to fall,
Prithee, pluck up a good resolution
   To be cheerful and thankful for all.

## THE CHILD.

### By the late John Briggs.

See the nurse her charge attending,
    Hear the darling's lisping prattle;
How its little eyes are blending
    O'er the pretty jingling rattle!

Quickly vexèd, soon appeasèd,
    Laughing, crying, waking, sleeping;
Chid and grievèd—kiss'd and pleasèd;
    All its cares express'd by weeping.

On the flower'd carpet playing,
    Sitting, creeping, rolling, lying,—
Now a sunny cheek displaying,—
    Now o'erspread with clouds, 'tis crying!

Sweetly wrapp'd in gentle slumber,—
    By its cot its mother watches;
Balmy kisses without number
    From its rosy cheeks she snatches.

We're but children, rather older,
    Puling in the lap of fashion;
Or, if aiming to be bolder,
    Tott'ring on the stilts of passion.

What's a coronet, if gain'd,
    But a *rush-cap*, or as awkward?
What's a carriage, when obtain'd?
    Nothing but a splendid *go-cart!*

We are children. Those who govern,
    Guardians, sent for our protection;
And the sceptre of the sovereign
    Is the ferula of correction.

Though we're infants,—to avow it
    Every *six-foot child* refuses;
Yet no name can please a poet
    Like "the elfin of the Muses."

## "THERE'S NO CHAP SHOULD EVER LOSE PLUCK."

### By Richard R. Bealey.

Aw'll try to be merry, aw will,
    Aw'll mak' up my mind on't to-day;
Though care is a rum 'un to kill,
    Aw'll feight, bu' aw'll have him away.

It's no use to simper an' sob,
    An' fret, because all isna' square,
It'll nobbut mak' worse a bad job,
    An' drive one reet into despair.

Then aw'll try to be merry, aw will,
    Aw'll laugh, an' aw'll dance, an' aw'll sing;
My spirit aw'm noan goin' to spill,
    To please oather parson or king.

Aw'd better by th' hauve goo to bed,
    An' sattle mysel' in a snooze,
Nor sit up an cry till my yed
    Feels as heavy as gamkeepers' shoes.

Aw'll smash that owd dule they co' th' dumps,
    An' gi'e him a sattlin' kick;
Aw ne'er knew him play "ace o' trumps;"
    He loses, wi nowt for a trick.

There's no chap should ever lose pluck;
    By th' mon, if he does, lad, he's lost;
He'll slither deawn th' hill loike a truck
    'Ut's gotten no break, in a frost.

There's nowt loike a will to foind th' way,
    An' nowt's hauve so strong as a try:
That's what my owd granny used t' say,
    An' granny ne'er towd me a lie.

## THE GARLAND OF LIFE.*

By the late J. B. Rogerson.

In youth we weave a garland of the brightest, fairest flowers,
Of buds of every scent and hue, from spring and summer bowers;
Then we revel in its fragrance, and we gaze with raptured eye,
And little think the loveliest flowers are earliest doom'd to die.
The primrose of our childhood soon outlives its little day,
The fragile snowdrop of our hopes will hasten to decay,
The daisy-buds of innocence all vanish from our view,
And the pure and modest violet droops its leaves of lustrous hue.


The tulip and the lilac-flower a little longer cling,
And the tendrils of the rose and pink abroad their beauty fling;
The vervain of enchantment, and the heart's ease, soon are gone,
Though the jasmine and the daffodil may yet a while live on.


The wall-flower, though it be the type of friendship in distress,
Falls from the wreath when come the days of pain and wretchedness;
The acacia, with its friendly buds, forsakes the hour of gloom,
And the honeysuckle fadeth with its incense and its bloom.

We gaze upon the garland with a sad and tearful eye,
And muse upon the wither'd leaves that all about it lie ;
They greet us as the emblems of our sorrow and despair,
And still hang around the willow-boughs that form'd the garland fair.

One only flower survives the buds of summer and of spring,
And telleth the repining heart that it to hope must cling ;
The blessed amaranthine flower a boon to man was given,
To speak of immortality, and point the way to heaven.

---

* The language of flowers, and emblematic garlands, are of very ancient date. The following are the definitions of the flowers alluded to: —The Primrose, childhood ; Snowdrop, hope ; Daisy, innocence ; Violet, modesty ; Tulip, declaration of love ; Lilac, first emotions of love ; Rose, love ; Pink, pure love ; Vervain, enchantment ; Heart's Ease, think of me ; Jasmine, amiableness ; Daffodil, self-love ; Wall-flower, fidelity in misfortune ; Acacia, friendship ; Honeysuckle, generous and devoted affection ; Dead Leaves, sadness and melancholy ; Weeping Willow, mourning ; Amaranth, immortality.—J. B. R.

## THE TOPER'S PLEA FOR DRINKING.

### BY THE LATE REV. THOMAS WILSON, B.D.[*]

If life, like a bubble, evaporates fast,
We must take off our wine, and the bubble will last;
For a bubble may soon be destroy'd with a puff,
If it is not kept floating in liquor enough.

If life's like a flower, as grave moralists say,
'Tis a very good thing, understood the right way;
For if life's like a flower, even blockheads can tell
If you'd have it look fresh, you must water it well.

That life is a journey no mortal disputes,
So their brains they will liquor instead of their boots;
And each toper will own, on life's road as he reels,
That a spur in the head is worth two on the heels.

If life's like a lamp, then, to make it shine brighter,
They assign to Madeira the post of lamplighter
They cherish the flame with Oporto so stout,
And drink ardent spirits till fairly burnt out.

This life to a theatre liken'd has been,
Where each has assign'd him a part in the scene;
If 'tis theirs to be tipsy, 'tis matter of fact,
That the faster they guzzle the better they act.

Life, 'tis said, like a dream or a vision appears,
Where some laugh in their slumbers, and others shed tears;
But of topers, when waked from their dream, 'twill be said,
That the tears of the tankard were all that they shed.

---

[*] Thomas Wilson was born at the village of Priest Hutton, near Lancaster, on the 3d December 1747. He died 3d March 1813, aged sixty-five. He was rector of Claughton, incumbent of the parochial churches of Clitheroe and Downham, head master for thirty-eight years of the Free Grammar School of Clitheroe, and a justice of peace for the county.

## "HEAW QUARE IS THIS LOIFE!"

### By Thomas Brierley.*

HEAW quare is this loife!   Could we live upo' love,
Time, wingèd wi' lilies, would fly loike a dove;
As it is, why i' th' midst of eawr smoiles an' content,
In comes the lonlort demandin' his rent.

In the midst uv eawr gaiety, frolic, an' tawk,
In the midst of the rosiest, busiest walk,
By a garden o' fleawers that a foo' would elate,
The stomach will whisper it wanteth some meight.

By a dell, where the sangsters are werblin' above,
An' every rich hawthorn is braided wi' love,
By a fountain, the clearest that naytur con make,
Yoar teeth, oh, yoar teeth in a second con ache.

Yoa may walk wi' a friend, yoa may leighn on his arm,
Yoa may think that that friend in his hert has no harm,
Yoa may swear that he's honest, ah me! very good;
That *friend's* happen slander'd yoa o 'at he could.

You may sit wi' yoar woife, yoa may gaze in her eyes,
Yoa may think they look very loike stars up i' th' skies,
Yoa may doat on yoar mate as a kitlin loves play;
An' yet, so admoired, hoo mun droop un' decay.

Yoa may think yoa'll be quiet, some solitude claim,
That for once i' yoar loife yoa'll indulge in a dream;
I' th' midst o' yoar castles   oh dear, not a bliss,
This toime 'tis yoar little un wantin' a kiss.

Yoa may tawk uv the future, wi seigh i' yoar hert,
Yoa may think that the world connut gi'e yoa a smart,
Yoa may love yoar dear childer, as birds love th' spring;
Yet deoth con fly off wi' their souls on his wing.

---

* Mr Thomas Brierley is a silk-weaver at Alkrington, near Middleton.

## HUMAN BROTHERHOOD.

### (FROM "AUTUMN LEAVES.")

### By John Critchley Prince.

The king who is swathed in the splendours of state,
    Whose power and possessions are wide,
Is akin to the beggar who whines at his gate,
    Howe'er it may torture his pride:
He is subject to ailments, and dangers, and woes,
    As the wretch who encounters the blast,
And, despite of his grandeur, his bones must repose
    In the same grave of nature at last.

The beauty, surrounded by homage and wealth,
    Whose glance of command is supreme,
Who walks in the grace of rich raiment and health,
    Whose life seems a musical dream,
Is sister to her, who, old, haggard, and worn,
    Receives a chance crust by the way;
The proud one may treat her with silence and scorn,
    But their kinship no truth can gainsay.

The scholar, who glories in gifts of the mind,
    Who ransacks the treasures of time;
Who scatters his thoughts on the breath of the wind,
    And makes his own being sublime;
Even he is a brother to him at the plough,
    Whose feet crush the flowers in their bloom;
And to him who toils on, with a care-furrow'd brow,
    In chambers of clangour and gloom.

Chance, circumstance, intellect, change us in life,
    Repulse us, and keep us apart;
But would we had less of injustice and strife,
    And more of right reason and heart!
One great human family, born of one Power,
    Each claiming humanity's thought—
We should let our best sympathies flow like a dower,
    And give and receive as we ought.

## THE GOOD SPIRIT.

### By Mrs G. Linnæus Banks.

Of all the good spirits that brighten the earth,
   Good temper is surely the best;
And luckless the hearth where she's seldom at home,
   Or comes but a casual guest;
Where the plumage is torn from her delicate wings,
And little is thought of the blessings she brings.

Good temper can give to the lowliest cot
   A charm with the palace to vie,
For gloomy and dark is the loftiest dome
   Unlit by her radiant eye;
And 'tis she who alone makes the banquet divine,
Gives for viands ambrosia, and nectar for wine.

The world would be dreary and barren indeed,
   Our pilgrimage weary and sad,
Did the strife-seeking spirit of Sullenness reign,
   To trample on hearts that were glad;
He would blot out life's sunshine, and pluck up its flowers,
Driving Hope's sweetest song-birds away from its bowers.

Alas! that we ever should fall 'neath a sway
   So tyrannous, cruel, and stern—
Should wilfully chase fair Good Temper away,
   Her favours indignantly spurn;
For with her there is pleasure, and gladness, and light;
With Sullenness, discord, and sadness, and night.

Let who will, give the demon a place in his breast,
   May Good Temper preside over mine;
She will lighten my sorrows, and whisper to Care
   Fewer thorns in my chaplet to twine:
Then, be mine this Good Spirit who comes at our call,
And would come, were she welcome, to each and to all!

## THE SUN AND THE FLOWERS:

### A SONG OF LIFE.

BY JAMES WATSON, "The Doctor."*

The sun the early morn doth greet;
    The dew begems the ground;
The flowers with fragrant odours meet,
    And perfume all around.

So enters man life's giddy maze,
    Fearless of future harms;
Pleasure her wily path displays,
    And lures him by her charms.

The sun pursues his eager flight,
    The dewdrops soon are fled;
Each flower, obedient to the light,
    Bends low its drooping head.

So thoughtless man, his hopes to win,
    In pleasure's labyrinth strays,
Till disappointment rushes in,
    And blights his future days.

---

\* James Watson was born in Manchester in 1775. He was for a short time at the Free Grammar School there. As a youth he became stage-struck, associated with George Frederick Cooke when in Manchester, and other kindred spirits, and became intemperate. He was by turns an apothecary, an actor, librarian at the Portico, usher in a school at Altrincham, &c., and was drowned in the Mersey, near Didsbury, on the 24th June 1820. While an apothecary, his friends gave him the sobriquet of "The Doctor." The late D. W. Paynter published a volume of Watson's poems in 1820, to which he prefixed a memoir of the poet, and entitled the book "The Spirit of the Doctor."

## SONG OF THE EXILE.

### By the late Rev. Richard Parkinson, D.D.

Farewell the shores I long have loved,
    The land where I have roam'd so long,
Where first my boyish heart was moved,
    That gave me birth and taught me song;
To mountain heath, and stream, and dell,
And loveliest home, a long farewell!

And farewell every tender tie
    That binds to life the wayward heart;
The soothing tongue, the gentle eye,
    The open brow, the winning art,
That drive the clouds of sorrow by,
And swell delight to ecstasy.

My loved companions—some will shed
    A tear for my unpitying doom,
And some forget me, with the dead
    Of ages in the silent tomb:
The tomb would be a happier lot—
I should not *know* myself forgot!

Where'er I roam, whate'er I see,
    Though fair and splendid be the scene,
Its splendour has no charms for me,
    Unless it tells of what hath been;
And then it wrings my bosom's core,
To think that it shall be no more!

This vast interminable plain
    My labouring eye with sorrow fills;
These waving seas of yellow grain
    Delight not like my native hills,
With darkly-frowning forests bound,
And with the heath's sweet blossom crown'd.

Oh! death is but a dreamless sleep—
    Or gladly would I couch my head,
Where I shall cease to watch and weep,
    In slumber with the unhallow'd dead;
For when asleep, in visions bland,
I see once more my native land!

## THINK NOT OF FAILURE.

(FROM "SONGS OF MY LEISURE HOURS.")

### BY MRS WM. HOBSON.

THINK not of failure,
　Look hopefully on;
Droop not o'er sorrows
　Whilst joy may be won;
Cease useless pining,
　Be up and astir,
Look boldly round thee,
　At fate ne'er demur.

Think not of stopping,
　Because in the strife
Some gain before thee
　The battle of life;
Let it awake thee
　To what may be won;
Let it arouse thee
　To what may be done.

Think not of casting
　Thy soul's dream away,
Because the road's rugged,
　And dreary the day;
Clear the mountain crest
　With the eagle's eye,
Its summit surmount
　Though it pierce the sky.

Think not that shadows
　For ever will rest;
Sunshine *must* follow—
　Hope on for the best.
Life has its beauty,
　Its summer and flowers,
To cheer with their light
　The dreariest hours!

## A WELCOME.

### By James Dawson, Jun.

Eh, Jone, aw 'm rare un' fain thae 'rt come,
    Thae 's had thi back to th' leet, aw 'm sure ;
Thae has no' bin this dur within
    These hawve-a-dozen years, or moor ;
Aw 'm fain, aw say, for t' see thee here,
    Owd brid ! an' heaw art getting on ?
Aw have no' seen thoose roguish een
    This mony a weary winter gone.

Thae favvert, then, a feightin' cock,
    Bo' neaw thae 'rt loike a mopin' hen ;
An' next, thae 'll be like some owd clock
    'At 's stopt, an' winno go agen ;
Thae 'rt lookin' wur for th' wear, for sure ;
    Bo' thae 'rt so loike, for owt aw know,
Thae 's bin i' th' meawt, aw dunno deawt ;
    Come, sit thee deawn an' tell me o.

This mornin', when I lee i' bed,
    Aw thowt, "Well, Jone 'll come to-neet ;"
An' this owd heart, ut 's fought an' bled,
    Beawnc't loike a bo, an' felt as leet !
Aw 'd rayther ha' thee i' mi heawse
    Than owt i' th' lord or lady line ;
Ther 's moor i' th' fruit than what 's i' th' root—
    I' deeds than names, tho' ne'er so fine.

Eawr Moll 's gone deawn to th' Ferny Bank,
    Eawr Robin 's eawt a cooartin' Nell ;
Pu' up thi chear to th' fender here,
    We 'n th' heawse an' th' har'stone to ussel ;
It 's rare an' grand an' comfortin',
    When folk are getten owd an' lone,
For t' have, rent free, like thee an' me,
    A heawse an' harbour o' ther own.

Bur come ; aw 'm howdin' back thi tale ;
    Aw know thae has one, good or bad,—
Some rare owd yarn for t' taych an' warn,
    Let 's yer thi seawnd thi keigh-note, lad ;
An' tell me, while thae 'rt wiftin' on,
    Heaw things are deawn i' Howden Dale,
An heaw thae 's peck'd sin th' trade wur wreck'd,
    An' hearts an' looms began for t' fail ? *

---

\* This song was written in 1864. The writer is a working man, at Hartshead, near Ashton-under-Lyne.

## AVARICE.

### By the late Rev. Thomas Wilson, B.D.

WHAT man in his wits had not rather be poor,
    Than for lucre his freedom to give ?
Ever busy the means of his life to secure,
    And for ever neglecting to live !

Environ'd from morning to night in a crowd,
    Not a moment unbent or alone ;
Constrain'd to be abject, though ever so proud,
    And at every one's call but his own.

Still repining and looking for quiet each hour,
    Yet studiously plying it still ;
With the means of enjoying such wish in his power,
    But accursèd in wanting the will.

For a year must be pass'd, or a day must be come,
    Before he has leisure to rest ;
He must add to his store this or that petty sum,
    And then he 'll have time to be blest.

But his gains, more bewitching the more they increase,
    Only swell the desires of his eye : —
Such a wretch let my enemy live, if he please,
    But, oh, not so wretchedly die !

## LINES WRITTEN IN A BOAT.

### By the late Rev. Richard Parkinson, D.D.

Pull! pull! my boys, the stream runs fast,
    And favouring is the gale;
And see, the setting sun has cast
    A shadow o'er the vale;
Our course is rough, the way is long,
    The light is sinking fast,
Pull! pull! my boys, your oars are strong,
    And favouring is the blast.

How bounds the boat beneath each stroke
    The labouring arm applies!
How, by the dashing oars awoke,
    The air-blown bubble flies!
How sweet, as on its wat'ry wings,
    The steady pinnace glides,
To listen to the stream that sings,
    And ripples round its sides!

Fast flies on either hand the bank,
    As down the stream we bound;
How soon yon towering mountain sank
    Beneath the swelling ground!
See on that hillock's verdant brow
    The sun's last radiance quiver;
We turn this jutting point—and now—
    The beam is gone for ever!

So floats our life down Time's rough stream,
    Such is its constant motion;
And bubbles on the land will gleam
    Like bubbles on the ocean.
Then pull, my boys! the stream runs fast,
    The sun's last beam is shining,
And fix your steady anchor fast
    Before the day's declining.

## THE WEAVER OF WELLBROOK.

### By B. Brierley.*

Yo gentlemen o with yor heawnds an' yor parks,—
    Yo may gamble an' sport till yo dee ;
Bo a quiet heawse nook,—a good wife an', a book,
    Is mooar to the likins o' me—e.
        Wi' mi pickers an' pins,
        An' mi wellers to th' shins ;
      Mi linderins, shuttle, and yealdhook ;—
        Mi treddles an' sticks,
        Mi weight-ropes an' bricks ;—
      What a life !—said the wayver o' Wellbrook.

Aw care no' for titles, nor heawses, nor lond ;
    Owd Jone's a name fittin' for me ;
An' gie mi a thatch wi' a wooden dur latch,
    An' six feet o' greawnd when aw dee—e.—&c.

Some folk liken t' stuff their owd wallets wi' mayte,
    Till they're as reawnt an' as brawsen as frogs ;
Bo for me—aw'm content when aw've paid deawn mi rent,
    Wi' enoof t' keep mi up i' mi clogs—ogs.—&c.

An' ther some are too idle to use ther own feet,
    An' mun keawr an' stroddle i' th' lone ;
Bo when aw'm wheelt or carried—it'll be to get berried,
    An' then Dicky-up wi' Owd Jone—one.—&c.

Yo may turn up yor noses at me an' th' owd dame,
    An' thrutch us like dogs agen th' wo ;
Bo as lung's aw con nayger aw'll ne'er be a beggar,
    So aw care no' a cuss for yo o—o.—&c.

Then, Margit, turn reawnd that owd hum-a-drum wheel,
    An' mi shuttle shall fly like a brid ;
An' when aw no lunger can use hont or finger,
    They'n say—while aw *could* do aw *did—id.*—&c.

---

    * The graphic writer in dialect of "Daisy Nook," the "Chronicles of Waverlow," (from which this song is taken,) "The Layrock of Langley Side," and "Tales and Sketches of Lancashire Life," &c.

## THE LESSON OF THE LEAVES.

### By Mrs G. Linnæus Banks.

    Glancing in the sunlight,
      Dancing in the breeze,
    See the new-born leaflets
      On the summer trees:
    Joying in existence,
      Whisp'ringly they play,
    Toying with each other
      Through the golden day:
    And when evening's eyelids
      Close upon the hill,
    Casting loving glances
      On the answering rill:
    Thus they dance and flutter
      All the summer through,
    Light, and gay, and gladsome,
      Leaflets green and new:
" Life is all before us—life is full of glee!"
Is the joyous chorus heard from every tree.

    Hanging in the branches,
      Drooping in the shade,
    Mark the autumn leaflets
      How they pine and fade;
    Rustling—as the storm-blast
      Sweeps across the moor—
    Driven by the whirlwind
      To the cottar's door;
    Dark, and thick, and heavy,
      With the dust of Time,
    Weary of existence,
      List their wintry chime,
    As the mournful cadence
      Rings in human ears,
    A never-ending moral
      For the coming years,
This the parting chorus—" Leaves, our course is run;
Death is now before us—but *our work is done!*"

## "MY *PIECE* IS O BU' WOVEN EAWT."

### BY RICHARD R. BEALEY.

My "piece" is o bu' woven eawt,
    My wark is welly done:
Aw've "treddled" at it day by day,
    Sin' th' toime 'ut aw begun.
Aw've sat i' th' loom-heawse long enough,
    An' made th' owd shuttle fly;
An' neaw aw'm fain to stop it off,
    An' lay my weyvin' by.


Aw dunnot know heaw th' piece is done;
    Aw'm fear'd it's marr'd enough;
Bu' th' warp wern't made o' th' best o' yarn,
    An' th' weft were nobbut rough.
Aw've been some bother'd neaw an' then
    Wi' knots, an' breakin's too;
They'n hamper'd me so mich at toimes
    Aw've scarce known what to do.


Bu' th' Mester's just, an' weel He knows
    'Ut th' yarn were none so good;
He winna' "bate" me when He sees
    Aw've done as weel's aw could.
Aw'se get my wage—aw'm sure o' that;
    He'll gi'e me o 'ut's due,
An', mebbe, in His t'other place,
    Some better wark to do.


Bu' then, aw reckon, 'tisn't th' stuff
    We'n getten t' put i' th' loom,
Bu' what we mak' on 't, good or bad,
    'Ut th' credit on 't 'll come.
Some wark i' silk, an' other some
    Ha'e cotton i' their gear;
Bu' silk or cotton matters nowt,
    If nobbut th' skill be theere.

Bu' now it's nee' to th' eend o' th' week,
    An' close to th' reckonin' day :
Aw 'll tak' my "piece" upon my back,
    An' yer what th' Mester 'll say :
An' if aw nobbut yer His voice
    Pronounce my wark "weel done,"
Aw 'll straight forget o th' trouble past
    I' th' pleasure 'ut 's begun.

## HOPE AND PERSEVERANCE.

### By John Critchley Prince.

Strive on, brave souls, and win your way
    By energy and care,
Waste not one portion of the day
    In languor or despair ;
A constant drop will wear the stone,
    A constant effort clear
Your way, however wild and lone :
    Hope on and persevere !

Strive on, and if a shadow fall
    To dim your forward view,
Think that the sun is over all,
    And will shine out anew ;
Disdain the obstacles ye meet,
    And to one course adhere,
Advance with quick but cautious feet :
    Hope on and persevere !

Rough places may deform the path
    That ye desire to tread,
And clouds of mingled gloom and wrath
    May gather overhead ;
Voices of menace and alarm
    May startle you with fear ;
But faith has a prevailing charm :
    Believe and persevere !

## OUR DAILY PATHS.*

### By Mrs Hemans.

> "Nought shall prevail against us, or disturb
> Our cheerful faith that all which we behold
> Is full of blessings."
> Wordsworth.

There's beauty all around our paths, if but our watchful eyes
Can trace it 'midst familiar things, and through their lowly guise;
We may find it where a hedge-row showers its blossoms o'er our way,
Or a cottage window sparkles forth in the last red light of day.

We may find it where a spring shines clear beneath an aged tree,
With the foxglove o'er the water's glass, borne downwards by the bee;
Or where a swift and sunny gleam on the birchen stems is thrown,
As a soft wind playing parts the leaves, in copses green and lone.

We may find it in the winter boughs, as they cross the cold, blue sky,
While soft on icy pool and stream their pencill'd shadows lie,
When we look upon their tracery, by the fairy frost-work bound,
Whence the flitting red-breast shakes a shower of crystals to the ground.

---

\* The admiration which the late Mr Dugald Stewart always expressed for Mrs Hemans's poetry was mingled with regret that she so generally made choice of melancholy subjects; and he sent her, through a friend of both, a message suggestive of his wish that she would employ her fine talents in giving more consolatory views of Providence, rather than dwell on the painful and depressing. In reply, Mrs Hemans sent to the friend the above piece, requesting it might be given to Mr Stewart, to whom it was read by his daughter. He was much charmed and gratified; and some of its lines were often repeated to him during the few remaining weeks of his life.

Yes! beauty dwells in all our paths—but sorrow too
 is there;
How oft some cloud within us dims the bright, still
 summer air!
When we carry our sick hearts abroad amidst the
 joyous things,
That through the leafy places glance on many-colour'd
 wings.

With shadows from the past we fill the happy wood-
 land shades,
And a mournful memory of the dead is with us in the
 glades;
And our dream-like fancies lend the wind an echo's
 plaintive tone
Of voices, and of melodies, and of silvery laughter
 gone.

But are we free to do even thus—to wander as we
 will—
Bearing sad visions through the grove, and o'er the
 breezy hill?
No! in our daily paths lie cares, that ofttimes bind
 us fast,
While from their narrow round we see the golden day
 fleet past.

They hold us from the woodlark's haunts, and violet
 dingles, back,
And from all the lovely sounds and gleams in the
 shining river's track;
They bar us from our heritage of spring-time, hope,
 and mirth,
And weigh our burden'd spirits down with the cum-
 bering dust of earth.

Yet should this be? Too much, too soon, despond-
 ingly we yield!
A better lesson we are taught by the lilies of the field!
A sweeter by the birds of heaven, which tell us in their
 flight
Of One that through the desert air for ever guides
 them right.

Shall not this knowledge calm our hearts, and bid
 vain conflicts cease?
Ay, when they commune with themselves in holy
 hours of peace;

And feel that by the lights and clouds through which
  our pathway lies,
By the beauty and the grief alike, we are training for
  the skies!

## DO A GOOD TURN WHEN YOU CAN.

### By Charles Swain.

It needs not great wealth a kind heart to display,—
If the hand be but willing, it soon finds a way;
And the poorest one yet in the humblest abode
May help a poor brother a step on his road.
Oh! whatever the fortune a man may have won,
A kindness depends on the way it is done;
And though poor be our purse, and though narrow our
  span,
Let us all try to do a good turn when we can!

The bright bloom of pleasure may charm for a while,
But its beauty is frail, and inconstant its smile;
Whilst the beauty of kindness, immortal in bloom,
Sheds a sweetness o'er life, and a grace o'er the tomb!
Then if we enjoy life, why, the next thing to do,
Is to see that another enjoys his life too;
And though poor be our purse, and though narrow our
  span,
Let us all try to do a good turn when we can!

## HELP ONE ANOTHER.

### By Thomas Brierley.

Slur on one another through life,
  Save om'dy* fro bangs that yo con,
Help folk wi' thur sledges along,
  Un' do it wi' th' heart of a mon;
Beware uv th' noddles un' cracks,
  Un' always give honest advice;
For life has a meanderin' track,
  Through rindles un' rivers uv ice.

Tak' note if it's brittle un' weak,
  Tak' note if it's slippy un' thin,
Tak' note if it's rotten un' rough,
  For happen the ice may let in;
Tak' note uv the jags un' the points,
  Un' if thur's a treacherous dot,
Be shure to point to o others
  That very same dangerous spot.

Tak' care uv the windin' un' turns,
  Tak' care uv the mazes that meet,
Un' always cry out i' good time,
  Wheer men connot ston o' thur feet;
Beware if it happens to thaw,
  When th' wayter comes trickling deawn,
For th' ice will impair in its strength,
  Un' theawsands are sartain to dreawn.

But recollect weel that the best
  Can never be always i' th' reet;
Th' wisest of men mun sometimes
  Be startled, un' slip off thur feet;
'Tis best to prepare then i' time,
  Un' give earthly bubbles thur due;
We'st never get through every slur,
  Witheawt an odd tumble or two.

---

\* Anybody.

If we tak' prudent care uv eawrsels,
  If we help other folk when we con,
If we stick to a friend when he's gull'd,
  Un' give him another lift on;
If we toss an old bite to distress,
  If we hond a good shirt to the poor,
If we strain every nerve for true worth,
  We're doin' what's reet, un' no moor.

## THE SONG OF OTHER DAYS.

### By Robert Rockliff.

Oh! sing it not, that simple air,
Though sung by one so young and fair,
Awakes no feeling save despair—
              Oimé!

For every note recalls the time
When first I listen'd to its chime,
And life and love were in their prime—
              Oimé!

I heard it on my bridal day,
And felt the happier for a lay
At once so tender and so gay—
              Oimé!

But death has taken from my side
The fondly loved and loving bride,
Who sang it in that hour of pride—
              Oimé!

And now the sweetest songs appear
Unto my disenchanted ear
A discord, which I loathe to hear—
              Oimé!

And even in this simple air,
Though sung by one so young and fair,
There breathes no feeling save despair—
              Oimé!

## SONGS OF THE PEOPLE.

### NO. I.—THE GATHERING. *

#### BY WILLIAM MORT.

HARK! to the hurried trampling
    Of the many thousand feet,
As they hasten to the rendezvous
    Along the crowded street!
No martial music heralds them,
    No lordling leads them on;
Their trumpets' notes are wild "hurrahs!"—
    Plumed chieftain they have none!

Yet firm are they in purpose
    From thraldom to be freed;
They have sworn a mighty oath to God,
    To battle for their creed!
And who, among created men,
    The dastard that would pause
Like her of Sodom, to *look back*
    In such a glorious cause!

No princely names possess they
    Their mission to support;
They have not sued to coronets,
    Nor bow'd and cringed at court.
They've pass'd the palace of the peer,
    And shunn'd its stately door,
Preferring welcome and a meal
    With the more noble poor.

And now once more they summon
    Their ill-clad ranks to meet;
The rude-made banners rise again,
    And sail along the street.
King! Lords! and Commons! ye shall hear
    What famish'd men can dare—
The voice of trampled slaves shall rise
    And echo through the air!

---

\* This was written in May 1834, and appeared thirty years ago in *Tait's Magazine*.

But, lo! Despair is with them—
    You may hear his hollow tread,
As vacantly he stalks along,
    And feebly mutters, " Bread ! "
And o'er his bony shoulder peers
    Dark Famine's sunken eye,
As with a mocking shout he lifts
    The gaudy flag on high!

Behold! they gain the platform—
    Their haggard chairman speaks;
Alas! he cannot varnish o'er
    That mute appeal, their cheeks!
Calmly he speaks, and calmly they
    Drink every burning word—
So still, betwixt each breathing pause
    A *whisper* had been heard!

Another rises—limbs deformed
    Support his wasted frame—
And long and loud and wild applause
    His proud success proclaim!
And lo! a third—well-favour'd he,
    And young, at least in years—
He speaks, and music falls to earth,
    And draws from *beggars* tears!

But vain their speeches—vain, alas!
    Bright gold would serve them more;
What can *their* feeble cries avail
    Beneath the full-fang'd boar?
As well, expecting bread, might they
    Go forth and ask a stone,
As seek redress from men whose hearts
    Are callous to their groan!

O ye who dress in purple robes,
    And daily eat a meal;
Who have no wrongs to be avenged,
    No starving pangs to heal;
Plead ye for those who have not gold
    To pay the pleader's fee;
And let it be no more a taunt,
    That *British men are free!*

## WELCOME WHITSUNTIDE.*

(FROM "SONGS OF MY LEISURE HOURS.")

### By Mrs Wm. Hobson.

WELCOME, with thy face of beauty;
   Welcome with thy joyous smile;
Pleasure beams around each duty
   When thy sunny hours beguile—
            Glowing Whitsuntide.

Welcome, with thy look of gladness
   Sparkling forth from every eye;
Where's the heart that's dimm'd with sadness
   When thou comest laughing by?
            Joyous Whitsuntide.

Welcome, with thy flowerets gemming
   Field and meadows, hill and dale,
Gleaming, round, rare pearl drops hemming
   O'er the forest and the vale—
            Jewell'd Whitsuntide.

Welcome, with thy form of brightness,
   And thy music-breathing tone;
Happiness and love and lightness
   Are the children of thy home—
            Laughing Whitsuntide.

Welcome, with thy life-breeze springing,
   Wafting round us health and joy;
To each care-worn spirit bringing
   Pleasures bearing no alloy—
            Freshening Whitsuntide.

Welcome, with thy pleasant rambles
   By the ocean and the stream,
Through the heath-wood and the brambles,
   Glowing as a poet's dream—
            Fairy Whitsuntide.

---

* Whitsuntide is the great yearly holiday of the working-classes of Lancashire.—ED.

Welcome, with thy laugh of childhood,
    Mingling with each zephyr's sigh ;
Ringing through the gladden'd wild-wood,
    Startling feather'd songsters nigh—
           Youthful Whitsuntide.

Welcome, with thy holy teaching,
    Weighty truths of nature's gold,
Bringing to our minds the preaching
    Of the patriarchs of old—
           Hallow'd Whitsuntide.

Welcome, with thy simple treasures,
    Violet and azure bell,
Coming to the heart as pleasures
    With a holy, heaven-wrought spell—
           Happy Whitsuntide.

Welcome, with thy youthful voices,
    Gaily singing from each glen :
How the inmost soul rejoices,
    Listening to thy strains again—
           Pleasant Whitsuntide.

Welcome, with thy scenes Elysian,
    Glowing landscapes rich and grand,
Like the pictures of some vision
    We have read of fairy land—
           Dreamy Whitsuntide.

Welcome, gladly do we greet thee,
    Holy, happy, regal time ;
And, with bounding hearts, we'll meet thee
    With a joyous, silvery chime—
           Welcome Whitsuntide.

## "BE KIND TO EACH OTHER!"

### By Charles Swain.

Be kind to each other!
   The night's coming on,
When friend and when brother
   Perchance may be gone!
Then 'midst our dejection,
   How sweet to have earn'd
The blest recollection
   Of kindness—*return'd!*
When day hath departed,
   And Memory keeps
Her watch—broken-hearted—
   Where all she loved sleeps.

Let falsehood assail not
   Nor envy disprove,—
Let trifles prevail not
   Against those ye love!
Nor change with to-morrow,
   Should fortune take wing;
But the deeper the sorrow
   The closer still cling!

    Oh, be kind to each other! &c.

## FAREWELL.

### BY THE LATE JOHN JUST.*

Soon we feel the sad impression;
   Soon the faltering tale we tell,
How each highly-prized possession
   Bids us all a long farewell.

Youth with all its envied pleasures,
   Broods o'er sorrows oft as well,—
Smiles an hour on what it treasures,
   Then for ever sighs farewell.

What avails a mother's feeling?
   Children's eyelids vainly swell;
Heart from heart the world is stealing:
   We must feel thy pangs—farewell!

High in hope and golden dreaming,
   Still at home we all would dwell;
Parting comes, and tears are streaming,
   Hot, wrung out by our farewell.

There's a youth just by yon dwelling,
   Wherein first his accents fell;
What emotions he is quelling
   As his hand waves his farewell!

Near the door there stands his mother,
   Mute with grief unspeakable,—
Sisters sobbing, and his brother
   Sunk in soul—at his farewell.

But, ah! who's she he now is meeting,
   Pale and sad, within the dell?
As 'twould break her heart is beating,—
   Keen as death is her farewell.

---

\* John Just, though a native of Natland, near Kendal, spent the best and most valuable part of his life at Bury and the neighbourhood. He was second master of the Bury Grammar School from 1832 till his death, on the 14th October 1852, in the fifty-fifth year of his age. He was an able geologist and chemist, an accomplished archæologist and antiquary, botanist, and philologist; and left many essays and papers in all these branches of science.

Fondest hopes she's long been rearing,
   Broken now's the illusive spell;
Far away her love is steering,
   And for ever's their farewell.

Mark an only child there dying,
   Low beneath the straw-roof'd cell;
Oh, what grief their souls are trying,
   While its parents weep—farewell!

Can a new-made bride feel sorrow,
   Join'd to him she loves so well?
Friends and home she quits to-morrow,
   Feels no joy in her farewell.

'Tis a trial past man's bearing,
   While slow sounds the funeral knell,
In her grave to leave, despairing,
   Her he loved, and look—farewell.

Constant as the day's returning,
   Lose we what we think excels;
Life's short span's a span of mourning,
   Fill'd with nought but sad farewells.

## STANZAS WRITTEN TO MUSIC.

By the late Rev. Richard Parkinson, D.D.

'Tis sadly sweet, in day's decline,
   To mark the waning sun,
And catch his last soft beams that shine
   When noonday hours are done:
And though more bright and glorious be
   His morning's glorious ray,
Yet dearer is his smile to me
   When evening dies away.

And so it is, as life declines,
   Each holier duty throws
A glory round our path, that shines
   More sweetly to the close.
And though the days of youth be bright,
   And manhood's hours be gay,
Yet cheering is our gentler light
   When evening dies away.

## FRIENDS DO NOT DIE.

(FROM "AFTER-BUSINESS JOTTINGS.")

### By Richard R. Bealey.

One cord more,
That bound my barque to this earthly shore,
        Is cut in twain.
O'er the sea
There is one voice more that calls to me,
        In loving strain.

Here on earth
There is one friend less that we deem'd of worth,
        And loved to know.
There above,
Is gone that friend, whom we still may love,
        Where we shall go.

'Tis not far
To the land where all those loved ones are;
        We feel it nigh.
Naught can part
Those who're united in the heart;
        Our friends don't die.

---

## "THERE ARE MOMENTS IN LIFE."

### By Charles Swain.

There are moments in life—though alas for their fleet-
    ness!—
  As brilliant with all that existence endears,
As if we had drain'd the whole essence of sweetness
  That nature intended should last us for years!
They pass—and the soul, as it swells with emotion,
  Believes that some seraph hath hallow'd the clime,
For never were pearls from the bosom of ocean
  So precious and dear as those moments of time!

That moment when hearts which have long been
    divided
  First meet, after absence hath tried them in vain;
Oh, years of affection, when *smoothly* they've glided,
  Can yield not a moment so blissful again;
When friends, that a word had estranged, have *forgiven*
  The word, and unite hand and heart as of old,
Oh, such moments of peace are like moments from
    heaven,
  They are gifts from a world which the angels behold!

## KINDLY WORDS.

(FROM "MISCELLANEOUS POEMS.")

### By J. C. Prince.

THE wild rose, mingled with the fragrant bine,
  Is calmly graceful, beautiful to me,
And glorious are the countless stars that shine
  With silent splendour over earth and sea;
But gentle words, and hearts where love has room,
  And cordial hands, that often clasp my own,
Are better than the fairest flowers that bloom,
  Or all the unnumber'd stars that ever shone.

The fostering sun may warm the fields to life,
  The gentle dew refresh the drooping flower,
And make all beauteous things supremely rife
  In gorgeous summer's grand and golden hour;
But words that breathe of tenderness and love,
  And genial smiles, that we are sure are true,
Are warmer than the summer sky above,
  And brighter, gentler, sweeter than the dew.

It is not much the selfish world can give,
  With all its subtle and deceiving art;
And gold and gems are not the things that live,
  Or satisfy the longings of the heart;
But oh! if those who cluster round the hearth
  Sincerely soothe us by affection's powers,
To kindly looks and loving smiles give birth,
  How doubly beauteous is this world of ours!

## ENGLAND'S DEAD.

### By Mrs Hemans.

Son of the ocean isle!
    Where sleep your mighty dead?
Show me what high and stately pile
    Is rear'd o'er glory's bed.

Go, stranger! track the deep,
    Free, free, the wild sail spread!
Wave may not foam, nor wild wind sweep,
    Where rest not England's dead.

On Egypt's burning plains,
    By the pyramid o'ersway'd,
With fearful power the noonday reigns,
    And the palm-trees yield no shade.

But let the angry sun
    From heaven look fiercely red,
Unfelt by those whose task is done!—
    *There* slumber England's dead.

The hurricane hath might
    Along the Indian shore,
And far by Ganges' banks at night
    Is heard the tiger's roar.

But let the sound roll on!
    It hath no tone of dread,
For those that from their toils are gone,—
    *There* slumber England's dead.

Loud rush the torrent floods
    The western wilds among,
And free in green Columbia's woods
    The hunter's bow is strung.

But let the floods rush on!
    Let the arrow's flight be sped!
Why should *they* reck whose task is done?—
    *There* slumber England's dead!

The mountain storms rise high
    In the snowy Pyrenees,
And toss the pine boughs through the sky,
    Like rose leaves on the breeze.

But let the storm rage on!
    Let the fresh wreaths be shed!
For the Roncesvalles' field is won,—
    *There* slumber England's dead.

On the frozen deep's repose,
    'Tis a dark and dreadful hour,
When round the ship the ice-fields close,
    And the northern night-clouds lower.

But let the ice drift on!
    Let the cold-blue desert spread!
*Their* course with mast and flag is done,—
    Even there sleep England's dead.

The warlike of the isles,
    The men of field and wave!
Are not the rocks their funeral piles,
    The seas and shores their grave?

Go, stranger! track the deep,
    Free, free, the white sail spread!
Wave may not foam, nor wild winds sweep,
    Where rest not England's dead.

## SONG FOR THE BRAVE.*

### By Samuel Bamford.

Say, what is the life of the brave?
   A gift which his Maker hath given,
Lest nothing but tyrant and slave
   Remain of mankind under heaven.
And what is the life of the brave,
   When staked in the cause of his right?
'Tis but as a drop to a wave—
   A trifle he values as light.

And what is the death of the brave?
   A loss which the good shall deplore;
His life unto freedom he gave,
   And free men behold him no more.
'Tis the close of a glorious day;
   'Tis the setting of yonder bright sun;
A summons that heralds the way
   To a heaven already begun!

And what is the fame of the brave?
   'Tis the halo which follows his day,
The noble examples he gave
   Remaining in splendid array!
The coward doth hopeless behold;
   The wise and the good do admire;
But in the warm heart of the bold
   Awakens a nobler fire!

Then who would not live with the brave?
   The wretch without virtue or worth.
And who would not die with the brave?
   The coward that cumbers the earth.
And who shall partake with the brave
   The fame which his valour hath won?
Oh, he that abides with the brave
   Till the battle of freedom is done.

## FAME.

### By Thomas Brierley.

There is a simple thing on earth,
　　That pleases nearly every one :
Its spring, or rise, or growth, or birth,
　　Was never yet determined on.
And men of sense and learning too,
　　Philosophers and poets warm,
Great warriors stern and patriots true,
　　Have striven hard to taste this charm.

'Tis nought to carry, nought to touch,
　　'Tis nought to view, 'twill nothing bless ;
'Twill not adorn, forsooth, e'en such
　　As wear it in its grandest dress.
'Tis tasteless, colourless, and thin,
　　'Tis never steady, never true ;
'Tis nought, and all the world to win,
　　And yet 'tis sweet as honey too.

'Tis like a primrose in the grass,
　　'Tis various as the new-cut blades,
It can be seen through just like glass,
　　And yet has many a thousand shades ;
'Tis fleeting as a sunny smile,
　　It can be grasp'd at many ways,
And scores have worn it for a while,
　　But not a mortal all his days.

What is this tasteless, honey food,
　　This brilliant rainbow, magic wand,
That's made a thousand warriors brood,
　　And slain so many poets grand ;
This never-to-be-finger'd gem,
　　This soul and pleasure-swealing flame,
This wreath and rosy diadem ?—
　　'Tis nought but bubbling, windy Fame !

## THE TRIED AND TRUE.

### By Mrs George Linnæus Banks.

I pass unregarded the selfish and vain,
   Who proffer a favour and make it a debt;
For service so render'd comes loaded with pain,
   But true-hearted kindness I never forget.

From the butterfly friends who when summer was bright
   Flutter'd round me with offers I did not require,
I turn to the few who in winter's dark night
   Were true and devoted—gold tried in the fire.

Or when prostrate in sickness, disabled by pain,
   Surrounded by hirelings, unheeded I lay;
From paraded assistance I turn'd with disdain,
   But the true-hearted kind ones I ne'er can repay.

To these and these only will memory cling,
   For sympathy shown in look, action, or word;
And the waters of gratitude ever upspring
   In the heart's brimming fount, though they sparkle unheard.

The hand of the spoiler hath often been laid
   On the dear ones whose loss I must ever regret;
But the true friends I tried in those seasons of shade,
   Are embalm'd in a heart which can *never* forget.

## THE PASS OF DEATH.

(WRITTEN SHORTLY AFTER THE DECEASE OF THE RIGHT
HON. GEORGE CANNING.)

### By Samuel Bamford.

Another's gone, and who comes next,
    Of all the sons of pride?
And is humanity perplex'd
    Because this man hath died?
The sons of men did raise their voice,
    And crièd in despair,
"We will not come, we will not come,
    Whilst Death is waiting there!"


But Time went forth, and dragg'd them on
    By one, by two, by three;
Nay, sometimes thousands came as one,
    So merciless was he!
And still they go, and still they go,
    The slave, the lord, the king;
And disappear, like flakes of snow,
    Before the sun of spring!


For Death stood in the path of Time,
    And slew them as they came;
And not a soul escaped his hand,
    So certain was his aim.
The beggar fell across his staff,
    The soldier on his sword,
The king sank down beneath his crown,
    The priest beside the Word.

And Youth came in his blush of health,
    And in a moment fell ;
And Avarice, grasping still at wealth,
    Was rollèd into hell ;
And Age stood trembling at the pass,
    And would have turn'd again ;
But Time said, " No, 'tis never so,
    Thou canst not here remain."

The bride came in her wedding-robe—
    But that did nought avail ;
Her ruby lips went cold and blue,
    Her rosy cheek turn'd pale !
And some were hurried from the ball,
    And some came from the play ;
And some were eating to the last,
    And some with wine were gay.

And some were ravenous for food,
    And raised seditious cries ;
But, being a "legitimate,"
    Death quickly stopt their noise !
The father left his infant brood
    Amid the world to weep ;
The mother dièd whilst her babe
    Lay smiling in its sleep.

And some did offer bribes of gold,
    If they might but survive ;
But he drew his arrow to the head,
    And left them not alive !
And some were plighting vows of love,
    When their very hearts were torn ;
And eyes that shone so bright at eve
    Were closèd ere the morn !

And one had just attain'd to power,
    He wist not he should die ;
Till the arrow smote his stream of life,
    And left the cistern dry !

Another's gone, and who comes next,
    Of all the sons of pride?
And is humanity perplex'd,
    Because this man hath died?

And still they come, and still they go,
    And still there is no end,—
The hungry grave is yawning yet,
    And who shall next descend?
Oh! shall it be a crownèd head,
    Or one of noble line?
Or doth the slayer turn to smite
    A life so frail as mine?

---

## FINIS.

### By Charles Swain.

Life's not our own—'tis but a loan
    To be repaid!
Soon the dark Comer's at the door,
The debt is due—the dream is o'er—
    Life's but a shade!

Thus all decline—that bloom or shine—
    Both star and flower;
'Tis but a little odour shed—
A light gone out—a spirit fled—
    A funeral hour!

Then let us show a tranquil brow,
    Whate'er befalls,—
That we upon Life's latest brink
May look on Death's dark face, and think
    An angel calls!

## V.
## Lays of the Cotton Famine.

IT would have been strange indeed if the vast distress throughout the cotton manufacturing districts of Lancashire in the years 1862, 1863, and 1864, should have been left unsung. The street-ballads of that period, on this sad subject, would fill a volume.

### THE MILL-HANDS' PETITION.

WE take extracts from a song by some "W. C.," printed as a street broadside at Ashton-under-Lyne, and sung in most towns of South Lancashire:—

> We have come to ask for assistance;
>   At home we've been starving too long,
> And our children are wanting subsistence;
>   Kindly aid us to help them along.

### CHORUS.

>   For humanity is calling,
>     Don't let the call be in vain;
>   But help us, we're needy and falling,
>     And God will return it again.

. . . . . .

> War's clamour and civil commotion
>   Has stagnation brought in its train;
> And stoppage brings with it starvation,
>   So help us some bread to obtain.

> The American war is still lasting;
>   Like a terrible nightmare it leans
> On the breast of a country, now fasting
>   For cotton, for work, and for means.

. . . . . . .

## THE FACTORY LASS.*

(FROM "PHASES OF DISTRESS: LANCASHIRE RHYMES.")

### BY JOSEPH RAMSBOTTOM.

O LADY, lady, stop a while,
   Until mi little tale aw 've towd;
To-day aw 've wandhert mony a mile,
   O'er teighrin' roads, i' th' weet an' cowd.
Ne'er shake your yead 'cose aw 'm ill-clad,
   For yo mistak mi aim, aw 'm sure;
Aw 'm noan a beggar—nowt so bad—
   Aw 're aye to' preawd, aw 'm neaw to' poor.

Aw 'm seechin' wark to help us thro':—
   Aw 'd scorn a beggar's cringin' part;—
Bo' sthrivin' hard an' clemmin' too,
   It welly breaks a body's heart.
Yo knawn what mills abeawt are stopt;
   An' beawt ther 's wark, what con one have?
Eawr two-three* things we 'n sowd or popt,†
   An' as for savin', we 'd nowt t' save.

My feyther deed some six yer sin',
   An' me an' mother then wur left;
For these last three mi mother 's bin
   O' th' use o' her reet arm bereft.
Mi wage sin' then, yo seen, 's kept two,
   An' so, yo 're sure we 'n had no fat;
We 'n ne'er complain'd, we 'n made it do;
   Bo' could we save owt eawt o' that?

. . . . . .

* We copy extracts from this and several other pieces from a volume having the above title, edited by "John Whittaker, a Lancashire Lad," who says:—" In the following poems, the author has given expression to the thoughts and feelings of the operatives of Lancashire, during the most terrible crisis through which they have ever passed. He possesses all the qualities requisite to enable him to do this successfully. He is as familiar with the various features of their everyday life as any one can be. His knowledge is not that of an outsider, who simply looks on at a new phase of life, and describes what he sees;—it is the knowledge possessed by one who is closely related to the people themselves, and who has himself shared their wants, their struggles, and their pleasures."

Owd folk betoimes are cross an' sore,
    An' speyken sharp when things are weel ;
So when they're clemmin' o th' day o'er,
    An' cripplet too, they're sure to feel.
Aw dunno' think hoo wants t' offend,
    Bo' being pitied maks her sore ;
Hoo sometimes thinks her arm 'ull mend,
    An' be just loike it wur before.

    .    .    .    .    .

Aw'm quite content 'ut th' facthory lass
    Shall bear her mother's weight o' care—
Shall help her when hard thrials pass,
    An' in her quiet pleasures share.
Neaw, lady, mi short tale aw've towd,
    If wark for wages yo can give,
Aw'd rayther have it than your gowd ;
    Aw 'll bless yo for it while aw live.

---

\* Two-three, *i.e.*, two or three.      † Pledged, pawned.

## "SHORT TIME, COME AGAIN NO MORE."

### (FROM A STREET BROADSIDE.)

OF this song of four verses, the first will suffice to indicate its character. It is a sort of parody on a well-known song :—

Let us pause in life's pleasures, and count its many tears,
    While we all sup sorrow with the poor ;
There's a song that will linger for ever in our ears,
    Oh, short time, come again no more !

### CHORUS.

It's the song of the factory operatives,
    Short time, short time, come again no more ;
For we can't get our cotton from the old Kentucky shore ;
    Oh, short time, short time, come again no more !

## THE SMOKELESS CHIMNEY.

By a Lancashire Lady,* (E. J. B.)

. . . . .

Traveller on the Northern Railway!
    Look and learn, as on you speed;
See the hundred smokeless chimneys;
    Learn their tale of cheerless need.

. . . . .

" How much prettier is this county!"
    Says the careless passer-by;
" Clouds of smoke we see no longer,
    What's the reason?—tell me why.

" Better far it were, most surely,
    Never more such clouds to see,
Bringing taint o'er nature's beauty,
    With their foul obscurity."

Thoughtless fair one! from yon chimney
    Floats the golden breath of life;
Stop that current at your pleasure!
    Stop! and starve the child—the wife.

Ah! to them each smokeless chimney
    Is a signal of despair;
They see hunger, sickness, ruin,
    Written in that pure, bright air.

" Mother! mother! see! 'twas truly
    Said last week the mill would stop;
Mark yon chimney, nought is going,
    There's no smoke from out o' th' top!

---

\* These stanzas were written by a lady in aid of the Relief Fund. They were printed on a card and sold, principally at the railway stations. Their sale, there and elsewhere, is known to have realised the sum of £160. Their authoress is the wife of Mr Serjeant Bellasis, and the only daughter of the late William Garnett, Esq. of Quernmore Park and Bleasdale, Lancashire.

"Father! father! what's the reason
　　That the chimneys smokeless stand?
Is it true that all through strangers,
　　We must starve in our own land?"

Low upon her chair that mother
　　Droops, and sighs with tearful eye;
At the hearthstone lags the father,
　　Musing o'er the days gone by.

Days which saw him glad and hearty,
　　Punctual at his work of love;
When the week's end brought him plenty,
　　And he thank'd the Lord above.

When his wages, earn'd so justly,
　　Gave him clothing, home, and food;
When his wife, with fond caresses,
　　Bless'd his heart, so kind and good.

Neat and clean each Sunday saw them,
　　In their place of prayer and praise,
Little dreaming that the morrow
　　Piteous cries for help would raise.

Weeks roll on, and still yon chimney
　　Gives of better times no sign;
Men by thousands cry for labour,
　　Daily cry, and daily pine.

Now the things, so long and dearly
　　Prized before, are pledged away;
Clock and Bible, marriage-presents,
　　Both must go—how sad to say!

Charley trots to school no longer,
　　Nelly grows more pale each day;
Nay, the baby's shoes, so tiny,
　　Must be sold, for bread to pay.

They who loathe to be dependent,
　　Now for alms are forced to ask;
Hard is mill-work, but believe me,
　　Begging is the bitterest task.

Soon will come the doom most dreaded,
    With a horror that appals;
Lo! before their downcast faces
    Grimly stare the workhouse walls.

Stranger, if these sorrows touch you,
    Widely bid your bounty flow;
And assist my poor endeavours
    To relieve this load of woe.

Let no more the smokeless chimneys
    Draw from you one word of praise;
Think, oh, think upon the thousands
    Who are moaning out their days.

Rather pray that, peace soon bringing
    Work and plenty in her train,
We may see these smokeless chimneys
    Blackening all the land again.

---

## "GOD BLESS 'EM, IT SHOWS THEY'N SOME THOWT!"

### By Samuel Laycock.

Is there nob'dy to thank these good folk?
    No poet, to scribble a line?
Aw wish aw could write yo' a song,
    Aw'd mak' yo' reet welcome to mine.
There's Waugh, he's bin writin' for years,
    An' mony a good tale, too, he's towd;
But he says nowt abeawt these bad times;
    Aw wonder, neaw, heaw he con howd.

Iv aw could draw pickturs loike him,
    An' ceawer deawn an' write hawve as weel,
Aw'd tell folk heaw thankful aw am;
    But aw couldn't tell th' hawve 'at aw feel.
When aw tak' up a papper to read,
    Aw can see theer heaw ready folk are
At helpin' poor creatures i' need,
    An' givin' us o they can spare.

We'n gentlemen, ladies, an' o,
   As busy i' th' country as owt,
Providin' for th' Lancashire poor;
   God bless 'em, it shows they'n some thowt!
Iv they'll only keep on as they do,
   We shall o be rigg'd eawt very soon;
There's one party givin' us frocks,
   An' another lot sendin' us shoon.

Th' Australians han sent us some gowd,
   To'rt feedin' an' clothin' o' th' poor;
An' they say it's noan o we mun have,
   For they're busy collectin' us moor.
An' th' Indians are helpin' an' o,
   Aw reckon they're grateful for th' past,
So they'll give us a bit ov a lift,
   For helpin' *them* eawt, when they'rn fast.

We'n clogs an' we'n clooas gan us neaw,
   There's boath second-honded an' new;
Some are givin' us soup twice a week,
   An' others are givin' us stew.
We're rare an' weel done to, aw'm sure,
   For we're fed, an' we're clothed, an' we're towt;
They pay'n us for gooin' to the schoo',
   An' gi'en us good larnin' for nowt.

God bless 'em for o 'at they've done,
   An' aw hope they'll keep doin' as well,
Till th' cleawd 'at hangs o'er's blown away,
   An' we're able to do for eawrsel'.
Excuse me for writin' these loines,
   For it's no use, aw conno' be still,
As long as they help us to live,
   *Aw'll* thank 'em, iv nob'dy else will.

## "CHEER UP A BIT LONGER."

### By Samuel Laycock.

Cheer up a bit longer, mi brothers i' want,
    There's breeter days for us i' store;
There'll be plenty o' tommy an' wark for us o,
    When this 'Merica bother gets o'er.
Yo'n struggled reet nobly, an' battled reet hard,
    While things han bin lookin' so feaw;
Yo'n borne wi' yor troubles an' trials so long,
    It's no use o' givin' up neaw.

    .    .    .    .    .    .

It's hard to keep clemmin' an' starvin', it's true;
    An' it's hard to see th' little things fret
Becose there's no buttercakes for 'em to eat;
    But we'n allus kept pooin' through yet.
As bad as toimes are, an' as feaw as things look,
    One's certain they met ha' bin worse;
For we'n getten a trifle o' summat, so fur,—
    It's only bin roughish, of course.

God bless yo, mi brothers, we're nobbut on th' tramp;
    We never stay long at one spot;
An' while we keep knockin' abeawt i' this world,
    Disappointments will fall to eawr lot;
So th' best thing we can do, iv we meon to get through,
    Is to wrastle wi' cares as they come;
Iv we're teighert an' weary,—well, let's never heed,
    We can rest us weel when we get whoam.

Cheer up, then, aw say, an' keep hopin' for th' best,
    An' things'll soon awter, yo'll see;
There'll be oachans o' butties for Tommy an' Fred,
    An' th' little uns perch'd on yor knee.
Bide on a bit longer, tak heart once agen,
    An' do give o'er lookin' soa feaw;
As we'n battled, an' struggled, an' suffer'd so long,
    It's no use o' givin' up neaw.

# FRETTIN'.

### By Joseph Ramsbottom.

Fro' heawrs to days—a dhreary length—
    Fro' days to weeks, one idle stonds,
An' slowly sinks fro' pride an' sthrength,
    To weeny heart and wakely honds.
An' still one hopes, an' ever thries
    To think 'ut betther days mun come;
Bo' th' sun may set, an' the sun may rise—
    No sthreak i' leet we find a-whoam!

    .    .    .    .    .    .

Aw want to see thoose days agen,
    To see folks earn whate'er they need;
O God! to think 'ut wortchin' men
    Should be poor things to pet 'un feed!
Ther's some to th' Bastile han to goo,
    To live o' th' rates they'n help'd to pay;
An' some get dow * to help 'em thro',
    And some are ta'en, or sent away.

    .    .    .    .    .    .

Whot is ther here, 'ut one should live,
    Or wish to live, weigh'd deawn wi' grief,
Thro' weary weeks an' months, 'ut give
    Not one short heawr o' sweet relief?
A sudden plunge, a little blow,
    At once 'ud eend mi care an' pain!
An' why noa do 't?—for weel aw know
    Aw lose bo' ills, if nowt aw gain.

Ay, why noa do it? It ill 'ud tell
    O' thoose wur left beheend, aw fear:
It's wrong, at fust, to kill mysel',
    An' wrong to lyev' mi childher here.
One's loike to tak some thowt for them—
    Some sort o' comfort one should give;
So one mun bear, an' starve, an' clem,
    An' pine, an' mope, an' fret, an' live.

---

\* Dole, relief from charity.

## TH' SHURAT WEAVER'S SONG.*

### By Samuel Laycock.

Confeaund it ! aw ne'er wur so woven afore,
Mi back's welly brocken, mi fingers are sore ;
Aw 've bin starin' an' rootin' among this Shurat,
Till aw 'm very near getten as bloint as a bat.

. . . . . .

Aw wish aw wur fur enough off, eawt o' th' road,
For o' weavin' this rubbitch aw 'm getten reet stow'd ;
Aw 've nowt i' this world to lie deawn on but straw,
For aw 've only eight shillin' this fortneet to draw.

Neaw aw haven't mi family under mi hat,
Aw 've a woife an' six childher to keep eawt o' that ;
So aw 'm rayther among it, at present, yo see :
Iv ever a fellow wur puzzled, it 's me !

Iv one turns eawt to steal, folk 'll co' me a thief,
An' aw conno' put th' cheek on to ax for relief ;
As aw said i' eawr heawse t' other neet to mi woife,
Aw never did nowt o' this soart i' mi loife.

---

\* During what has been well named "The Cotton Famine," amongst the imports of cotton from India, perhaps the worst was that denominated "Surat," from the city of that name, in the province of Guzerat, a great cotton district. Short in staple, and often rotten, bad in quality, and dirty in condition, (the result too often of dishonest packers,) it was found to be exceedingly difficult to work up ; and from its various defects, it involved considerable deductions, or "batings" for bad work, from the spinners' and weavers' wages. This naturally led to a general dislike of the Surat cotton, and to the application of the word "Surat" to designate any inferior article. One action was tried at the assizes — the offence being the applying to the beverage of a particular brewer the term of "Surat beer." Besides the song given above, several others were written on the subject.

Oh dear! if yond' Yankees could only just see
Heaw they're clammin' an' starvin' poor weavers loike me,
Aw think they'd soon settle their bother, an' strive
To send us some cotton to keep us alive.

There's theawsands o' folk just i' th' best o' their days,
Wi' traces o' want plainly seen i' their faze;
An' a future afore 'em as dreary an' dark,
For when th' cotton gets done we shall o be beawt wark.

We'n bin patient an' quiet as long as we con;
Th' bits o' things we had by us are welly o gone;
Mi clogs an' mi shoon are gettin' worn eawt,
An' mi halliday cloas are o on 'em " up th' speawt."

. . . . . .

Mony a toime i' mi days aw've seen things lookin' feaw,
But never as awkard as what they are neaw;
Iv there isn't some help for us factory folk soon,
Aw'm sure we shall o be knock'd reet eawt o' tune.

. . . . . .

## GOOIN' T' SCHOO'.

(FROM " PHASES OF DISTRESS—LANCASHIRE RHYMES.")

### By Joseph Ramsbottom.

Heaw slow these weary weeks drag on!
    Th' hard toimes 'ull ne'er be o'er, aw 'm sure;
Eawr mill's bin stondin' idle yon'
    For these last eighteen months, or mooar.
We walk abeawt i' the leet o' the day
    I' clooas 'ut som'dy else has bowt;
Think o'er it when an' heaw we may,
    We're like to own it's up to nowt.

To thrust to som'dy else for bread,
    An' by th' relief keep torin' on,
Maks honest folk to hang their yead,
    An' crushes th' heart o' th' preawdest mon.
We know'n it's not eawr bread we ate;
    We know'n they're not eawr clooas we wear;
We want agen eawr former state,
    Eawr former dhrudgin' life o' care.

    .    .    .    .    .

It's fro' no faut o' eawrs, it's true,
    An' folks han met eawr wants like men,
Like brothers and like sisters too,—
    May th' great God pay 'em back agen.
Heawe'er aw grum'le at mi state,
    Aw've no hard word to say to them;
Aw thank the poor, aw thank the great,
    'Ut couldno' stond to see us clem.

Their help has bin great help to me,
    It's that alone 'ut sent me t' schoo';
It's that 'ut towt me th' A B C,
    For o aw'd turnt o' forty-two.
'Twur rayther hard at fust to sit
    An' stare at things aw couldno tell,
'Cose when owt puzzl't me a bit,
    O th' lads 'ud lough among thersel'.

    .    .    .    .    .

On lots o' things aw get new leet,
    Mi idle toime 's noan badly spent ;
To the woife an' the childher neaw oitch neet
    Aw read a bit i' th' Testiment—
Heaw Jesus Christ once fed the poor,
    An' the little childher to Him co'd ;
Heaw th' sick an' blind He oft did cure,
    An' the lame, to help 'em on their road.

When o these weary toimes are past—
    When th' schoo's an' o are past away—
These happy neets a-whoam 'ull last,
    At th' eend o' mony a breeter day :—
Bo' th' eend o' th' ill it 's hard to see,
    An' very hard to battle thro' ;
A gradely plague it 's bin to me—
    It 's been a gradely blessin' too.

## HARD TIMES; OR, TH' WEYVUR TO HIS WIFE.

### By "a Lancashire Lad," (James Bowker.)

Draw up thy cheer, owd lass, we'n still a bit o' fire,
An' I'm starv't to deoth wi' cummin' throo th' weet an' mire;
He towd a lie o' thee an' me, as said as th' love o' th' poor
Flies out o' th' kitchen window, when clemmin' cums to th' door.
Aw'm not ruein'—as thae weel knows—as ever I wed thee,
But I've monny a quare thowt as thae mon sometimes rue o' me.

I'm mad at them America foos, as never hes enuff
O' quarrelin' an' strugglin', and sich unnat'rel stuff,
An' its ter'ble hard, owd wife, to ceawer bi' th' chimley jam,
An' think if they keep on feightin', as thee an' me mun clam;
An' not aar faut, its like breykin' wer shins o'er th' neighbours' stoos,
An' it shows us for one woise mon, ther's welly twenty foos.

But better chaps nor me an' thee hes hed to live o' nowt,
An' we'n hed a tidy time on't afoor th' war brok' out;
An' if I'm gerrin' varra thin, it matters nowt o' me,
Th' hardest wark is sittin' here schaming for th' choilt an' thee.
Tha'art gerrin' ter'ble pale too, but fowk wi' nowt to heyt
Con't luk as nice an' weel as them as plenty hes o' meyt.

Ther's lots o' hooams areawnd us whear wot they waste i' th' day,
'Ud sarve for thee an' th' choilt an' me, an' some to give away;
An' as I passes by their dooars, I hears their music sweet,
An' I con't but think o' thee till th' teears dim mi seet;
For if I'd lots o' brass, thae shud be diff'rent, never fear,
For th'art nooan so feaw, yet, wench, if thae'd gradely clooas to wear.

An' aar bonny little Annie, wi' her pratty een so breet,
Hoo shud sleep o' feathers, and uv angels dreom o neet;
I fancies I con see her monny a weary heawr i' th' day,
As I shud loike her to be sin, if luv mud heve its way;
And if what's i' this heart o' moine cud nobbut cum to pass,
Hoo shud bi' th' happiest woman, as hoo is th' bonniest lass.

I'm a foo wi' clammin' soa, or I shudn't toke like this,
It nobbut meks wer teeth watter to think o' sich like bliss;
An' th' winter cummin' on so fast, wi' th' dark, an' th' snow, an' th' cowd,
For I heeard th' robin sing to-day as I heeard him sing of owd,
When thee an' me wur younger, an' i' wur soft cooartin days,
An' I cum whistlin' thro' the fields to yoar owd woman's place.

Thea loved me then, an' as wimmen's soft enuff for owt,
I do believe thae loves me neaw, mooar nor ever I'd hae thowt,
An' tha' hes but one excuse, if I'm ragg'd, I'm fond o' thee,
An' times, though hard, I connot think 'll change thee or me,
For if we're true an' reet, an' as honest as we're poor,
We's never hev no wos chap nor poverty at th' dooar.

## VI.
## Sea Songs.

IF some gentle reader should wonder why sea songs are included in a volume of Lancashire songs and ballads, our answer to the unuttered query would be twofold:—First, because Lancashire is a maritime county, possessing in Liverpool the greatest commercial seaport in the world; and, secondly, because a few years ago we also had a local Dibdin in the benevolent and lamented Edward Rushton of Liverpool,[*] a few of whose songs we have obtained permission from his descendants to copy.

### WILL CLEWLINE.

A TALE OF THE PRESSGANG.

BY THE LATE EDWARD RUSHTON.

From Jamaica's hot clime and her pestilent dews;
   From the toil of a sugar-stow'd barque;
From the perilous boatings that oft thin the crews,
   And fill the wide maw of the shark;
From fever, storm, famine, and all the sad store
   Of hardships by seamen endured,
Behold, poor Will Clewline escaped, and once more
   With his wife and his children safe moor'd.

---

[*] The late Mr Edward Rushton was born at Liverpool in November 1756, and educated in the Free School there. While a sea apprentice, at the age of sixteen, on board a ship in a storm, when captain and crew left the vessel to drive at hazard, young Rushton seized the helm, called the men to their duty, and, under his direction, the vessel was saved; for which he received the thanks of captain and crew, was made second mate, and had a grateful endorsement on his indentures by the owners. While mate on board a slaver, all the slaves were seized with ophthalmia, and none but Rushton had the humanity to care for them; the result to himself was total blindness for thirty-three years. He partially recovered his sight in 1807, by the skill of Mr Gibson, oculist, Manchester. He distinguished himself by the promotion of every philanthropic object and institution in Liverpool, and his writings were largely instrumental in the establishment of the Liverpool Blind Asylum. He died in November 1814, aged fifty-three; leaving a son, Edward, barrister-at-law, and in the latter part of his life, stipendiary magistrate for the borough of Liverpool. Mr Rushton's poems have been twice published,—in 1806,—and posthumously in 1814, with a sketch of his life by the late Rev. Dr Shepherd, of Gateacre.

View the rapture that beams in his sun-embrown'd
    face,
  While he folds his loved Kate to his breast—
While his little ones, trooping to share his embrace,
    Contend who shall first be caress'd!
View them climb his loved knee, while each tiny heart
    swells,
  As he presses the soft rosy lip,
And of cocoa-nuts, sugar, and tamarinds tells
  That are soon to arrive from the ship!

Then see him reclined on his favourite chair,
  With his arm round the neck of his love,
Who tells how his friends and his relatives fare,
  And how the dear younglings improve.
The evening approaches, and round the snug fire
  The little ones sport on the floor—
When lo! while delight fills the breast of the sire,
  Loud thunderings are heard at the door.

And now, like a tempest that sweeps through the sky,
  And kills the first buds of the year—
Oh! view, 'midst this region of innocent joy,
  A gang of fierce hirelings appear.
They seize on the prey, all relentless as fate:
  He struggles—is instantly bound;
Wild scream the poor children, and lo! his loved Kate
  Sinks pale and convulsed to the ground.

To the hold of a tender, deep, crowded, and foul,
  Now view your brave seaman confined,
And on the bare planks, all indignant of soul,
  All unfriended, behold him reclined.
The children's wild screams still ring in his ear:
  He broods on his Kate's poignant pain;
He hears the cat hauling—his pangs are severe;
  He feels, but he scorns to complain.

Arrived now at Plymouth, the poor enslaved tar
  Is to combat for freedom and laws—
Is to brave the rough surge in a vessel of war:
  He sails—and soon dies in the cause.

Kate hears the sad tidings, and never smiles more,
    She falls a meek martyr to grief ;
His children, kind friends and relations deplore,
    But the parish alone gives relief.

Ye statesmen, who manage this cold-blooded land,
    And who boast of your seamen's exploits,
Ah! think how your death-dealing bulwarks are mann'd,
    And learn to respect human rights.
Like felons, no more let the sons of the main
    Be sever'd from all that is dear ;
If their sufferings and wrongs be a national stain,
    Oh, let the foul stain disappear.

## ABSENCE.

#### BY THE LATE EDWARD RUSHTON.

WHEN through the wild unfathom'd deep,
Wet with the briny spray, we sweep,
To Kate, to lovely Kate, and home,
My anxious thoughts unceasing roam.
Again I see her on the pier—
Again behold the falling tear;
Again I view her bosom swell,
And hear the sorrowing word "Farewell."

When all is calm, and the bleach'd sails
Are furl'd, or hanging in the brails,
The wide expanse of glassy sea,
And sky from cloudy vapours free,
While thoughtless o'er the side I lean,
Bring to my mind the placid mien
Of that dear girl whom I adore,
And left in tears on Albion's shore.

Or when the fierce tornadoes howl,
And nerve the fearless seaman's soul,
The towering surges, as they break,
Display the whiteness of her neck;
The petrels, too, that seem to tread
The foaming brine, with wings outspread,
Oft bring the ebon locks to mind
Of that dear girl I left behind.

When on my watch, the dawn full oft
Has shown those tints, so mild and soft,
That mark the lip and cheek of her
Whom I 'bove all the world prefer.
And thus, where'er the seaman goes,
'Midst torrid heat, or polar snows,
Some image still recalls to mind
The witching charms he leaves behind.

## THE NEGLECTED TAR.

### By the late Edward Rushton.

To ocean's sons I lift the strain,
    A race renown'd in story;
A race whose wrongs are Britain's stain,
    Whose deeds are Britain's glory.
By them, when courts have banish'd peace,
    Your sea-girt land's protected;
But when war's horrid thunderings cease,
    These bulwarks are neglected.

When thickest darkness covers all,
    Far on the trackless ocean;
When lightnings dart and thunders roll,
    And all is wild commotion;
When o'er the barque the foam-capt waves
    With boisterous sweep are rolling;
The seaman feels, yet nobly braves,
    The storm's terrific howling.

When long becalm'd on southern brine,
    Where scorching beams assail him;
When all the canvas hangs supine,
    And food and water fail him.
Then oft he dreams of that loved shore,
    Where joys are ever reigning;—
The watch is call'd,—his rapture's o'er,—
    He sighs, but scorns complaining.

Now deep immersed in sulphurous smoke,
    Behold him at his station;
He loads his gun, he cracks his joke,
    And moves all animation.
The battle roars, the ship's a wreck,
    He smiles amid the danger;
And though his messmates strew the deck,
    To fear his soul's a stranger.

Or, burning on that noxious coast,
  Where death so oft befriends him;
Or pinch'd by hoary Greenland's frost,
  True courage still attends him.
No clime can this eradicate,
  He glories in annoyance;
He, fearless, braves the storms of fate,
  And bids grim death dèfiance.

Why should the man who knows no fear
  In peace be thus neglected?
Behold him move along the pier,
  Pale, meagre, and dejected;
He asks a berth, with downcast eye,
  His prayers are disregarded;
Refused—ah! hear the veteran sigh,
  And say—are tars rewarded?

Much to these fearless souls you owe;
  In peace would you neglect them?
What say you, patriot souls? Oh no!
  Admire, preserve, protect them.
And oh! reflect, if war again
  Should menace your undoing,
Reflect who then would sweep the main,
  And shield your realm from ruin.

  CHORUS.—Then oh! protect the hardy tar;
    Be mindful of his merit;
    And if pure justice urge the war,
    He'll show his daring spirit.

———◆———

## THE LASS OF LIVERPOOL.

### By the late Edward Rushton.

Where cocoas lift their tufted heads,
   And orange-blossoms scent the breeze,
Her charms the mild Mulatto spreads,
   And moves with soft and wanton ease.
And I have seen her witching smiles,
   And I have kept my bosom cool;
For how could I forget thy smiles,
   O lovely lass of Liverpool!

The softest tint the conch displays,
   The cheek of her I love outvies;
And the sea-breeze, 'midst burning rays,
   Is not more cheering than her eyes.
Dark as the petrel is her hair,—
   And Sam, who calls me love-sick fool,
Ne'er saw a tropic bird more fair
   Than my sweet lass of Liverpool.

Though doom'd from early life to brave
   The feverish swamp and furious blast;
Though doom'd to face the foam-capt wave,
   And mount the yard and quivering mast;
Though doom'd to brave each noxious soil,
   And train'd in stern misfortune's school;
Yet still, oh! 'twould be bliss to toil
   For thee, sweet lass of Liverpool.

And when we reach the crowded pier,
   And the broad yards are quickly mann'd;
Oh! should my lovely girl be near,
   And sweetly smile, and wave her hand;
With ardent soul I'd spring to shore,
   And, scorning dull decorum's rule,
To my fond bosom o'er and o'er
   Would press the lass of Liverpool.

## "WHEN THE BROAD ARCH OF HEAVEN."

SONG—WRITTEN FOR THE ANNIVERSARY OF THE LANCASTER MARINE SOCIETY.

BY THE LATE EDWARD RUSHTON.

WHEN the broad arch of heaven is blue and serene,
    And the ocean reflects the bright day;
When, unswell'd by the breeze, the bleach'd canvas is seen,
    And the bows are unwash'd by the spray;
When the morn is thus smiling, each mariner knows,
    Who the perilous tempest oft braves,
That the loftiest barque, ere the day's dreadful close,
    May float a mere wreck on the waves.

So on life's changeful ocean, with souls all elate,
    And with prospects all placid and clear;
While fortune's soft gales on our efforts await,
    For wealth's flattering harbour we steer:
When lo! disappointment's dark vapours arise,
    And the winds of adversity roar;
And hope's towering canvas in tatters soon flies,
    And sorrow's wild waves whelm us o'er.

Since life's brightest azure may thus be o'ercast,
    And soon threatening clouds may appear;
Oh! 'tis wise to prepare for the soul-piercing blast,
    Ere you feel its destructive career.
Yes, ye men of old Lune, to the surge long inured,
    Oh! 'twas wise this fair harbour to form;
Where your dearest connexions may one day be moor'd,
    Unexposed to the pitiless storm.

At eve, when the little ones climb your loved knee,
    And the mother looks on with a smile,
When they prattle around you all frolic and glee,

  And soften the day's rugged toil ;
When you view the loved group with affection's strong
   glow,
  When you feel sensibility's tear ;
Oh ! reflect, men of Lune, that should death lay you
   low,
  Protectors and guardians are here.

And oft, when the petrel his dark wing displays,
  In the trough of the mountainous wave ;
When the craggy lee-shore is perceived through the
   haze,
  And the breakers all dreadfully rave ;
'Neath the vertical sun, when contagions arise,
  Or when battle the atmosphere rends ;
Oh ! with comfort reflect that your soul's dearest ties
  Shall here find protectors and friends.

## THE FAREWELL.

BY THE LATE EDWARD RUSHTON.

The shivering topsails home are sheeted,
    And cheerily goes the windlass round;
" Heave, heave, my hearts!" is oft repeated,
    And Mary sighs at every sound.
The yellow fever, scattering ruin;
    The shipwreck'd veteran's dying cries;
And war, the decks with carnage strewing—
    All, all before her fancy rise.

As bends the primrose, meek and lowly,
    All bruised by April's pelting hail;
So, while the anchor rises slowly,
    Poor Mary droops, distress'd and pale.
And oft, while at his handspike toiling,
    Full many a glance her seaman steals;
And oft he tries, by gaily smiling,
    To hide the parting pang he feels.

Now through the blocks the wind is howling—
    The pilot to the helmsman cries;
And now the bulky ship is rolling,
    And now aloft the sea-boy flies.
The whiten'd canvas swift is spreading,
    Around the bows the surges foam;
And many a female tear is shedding,
    And thoughts prevail for love and home.

Her tar, among the sunburnt faces,
    Now Mary views with fond regard;
Now o'er the deck his form she traces—
    Now, trembling, sees him on the yard.
Where'er he moves, alert and glowing,
    Her beauteous azure eyes pursue—
Those eyes that show, with grief o'erflowing,
    Like violets wet with morning dew.

Unmoved, 'midst regions wild and dreary,
   Poor Will had pass'd through woes severe ;
Yet now from far he views his Mary,
   And turns to hide a falling tear.
The biting winds blow strong and stronger,
   And the broad waves more wildly swell :
Will hears the boat can wait no longer,
   And springs abaft to bid farewell.

" O my sweet girl !" with strong emotion,
   The tar exclaims, " now—now—adieu !
I go to brave the changeful ocean,
   Yet thou shalt ever find me true."
With quivering lip and deep dejection,
   " Heaven shield my Will," she cries, " from harms."
His look bespeaks extreme affection,
   And now he locks her in his arms.

Again the boatmen, hoarsely bawling,
   Declare they cannot, will not stay ;
And though the crew the cat are hauling,
   Yet Will must see his love away.
Now at the side, expression ceases :
   She gains the skiff—she makes for land,
And 'twixt them, as the brine increases,
   They gaze, they sigh, they wave the hand.

## CASABIANCA.

[Young Casabianca, a boy about thirteen years old, son to the Admiral of the Orient, remained at his post (in the Battle of the Nile) after the ship had taken fire, and all the guns had been abandoned; and perished in the explosion of the vessel, when the flames had reached the powder.]

THE boy stood on the burning deck
   Whence all but he had fled;
The flame that lit the battle's wreck
   Shone round him o'er the dead.

Yet beautiful and bright he stood,
   As born to rule the storm—
A creature of heroic blood,
   A proud, though childlike form.

The flames rolled on—he would not go
   Without his father's word;
That father, faint in death below,
   His voice no longer heard.

He called aloud :—" Say, father, say
   If yet my task is done!"
He knew not that the chieftain lay
   Unconscious of his son.

" Speak, father!" once again he cried,
   If I may yet be gone!"
And but the booming shots replied,
   And fast the flames rolled on.

Upon his brow he felt their breath,
   And in his waving hair,
And looked from that lone post of death
   In still yet brave despair;

And shouted but once more aloud,
   " My father! must I stay?"
While o'er him fast, through sail and shroud,
   The wreathing fires made way.

They wrapt the ship in splendour wild,
   They caught the flag on high,
And streamed above the gallant child
   Like banners in the sky.

There came a burst of thunder-sound—
   The boy—oh! where was he?
Ask of the winds that far around
   With fragments strewed the sea!—

With mast, and helm, and pennon fair,
   That well had borne their part;
But the noblest thing which perished there
   Was that young faithful heart!

**MRS FELICIA HEMANS**

## A THOUGHT OF THE SEA.

My earliest memories to thy shores are bound,
Thy solemn shores, thou ever-chanting main !
The first rich sunsets, kindling thought profound
In my lone being, made thy restless plain
As the vast, shining floor of some dread fane,
All paved with glass and fire. Yet, O blue deep !
Thou that no trace of human hearts dost keep,
Never to thee did love with silvery chain
Draw my soul's dream, which through all nature sought
What waves deny,—some bower of *steadfast* bliss,
A *home* to twine with fancy, feeling, thought,
As with sweet flowers. But chastened hope for this
Now turns from earth's green valleys, as from thee,
To that sole changeless world, where "there is no more sea."

## DISTANT SOUND OF THE SEA AT EVENING.

Yet, rolling far up some green mountain-dale,
Oft let me hear, as ofttimes I have heard,
Thy swell, thou deep ! when evening calls the bird
And bee to rest ; when summer-tints grow pale,
Seen through the gathering of a dewy veil ;
And peasant-steps are hastening to repose,
And gleaming flocks lie down, and flower-cups close
To the last whisper of the falling gale.
Then 'midst the dying of all other sound,
When the soul hears thy distant voice profound,
Lone worshipping, and knows that through the night
'Twill worship still, then most its anthem-tone
Speaks to our being of the Eternal One,
Who girds tired nature with unslumbering might.

**MRS FELICIA HEMANS**

# NORTHERN CLASSIC REPRINTS

## The Manchester Man
(Mrs. G. Linnaeus Banks)
Re-printed from an 1896 illustrated edition — undoubtedly the finest limp-bound edition ever. Fascinating reading, includes Peterloo. Over 400 pages, wonderfully illustrated.
ISBN 1 872226 16 7 £4.95

## The Manchester Rebels
(W Harrison Ainsworth)
A heady mixture of fact and fiction combined in a compelling story of the Jacobean fight for the throne of England. Manchester's involvement and the formation of the Manchester Regiment. Authentic illustrations.
ISBN 1 872226 29 9 £4.95

## The Dock Road
(J. Francis Hall RN)
A seafaring tale of old Liverpool. Set in the 1860s, with the American Civil War raging and the cotton famine gripping Lancashire. Period illustrations.
ISBN 1 872226 37 X £4.95

## Stories & Tales Of Old Lancashire
(Frank Hird)
Over 70 fascinating tales told in a wonderful light-hearted fashion. Witches, seiges and superstitions, battles and characters all here.
ISBN 1 872226 21 3 £4.95

# NORTHERN CLASSIC REPRINTS

## Hobson's Choice (the Novel)
### (Harold Brighouse)
The humorous and classic moving story of Salford's favourite tale. Well worth re-discovering this enjoyable story. Illustrated edition. Not been available since 1917, never before in paperback.
ISBN 1 872226 36 1      £4.95

## Poems & Songs Of Lancashire
### (Edwin Waugh)
A wonderful quality reprint of a classic book by undoubtedly one of Lancashire's finest poets. First published 1859 faithfully reproduced. Easy and pleasant reading, a piece of history.
ISBN 1 872226 27 2      £4.95

## Stories and Tales Of Old Merseyside
### (Frank Hird, edited Cliff Hayes)
Over 50 stories of Liverpool's characters and incidents PLUS a booklet from 1890 telling of the city's history, well illustrated.
ISBN 1 872226 20 5      £4.95

## The Lancashire Witches
### (W. Harrison Ainsworth)
A beautifully illustrated edition of the most famous romance of the supernatural.

ISBN 1 872226 55 8      £4.95

## The Best of Old Lancashire — Poetry & Verse

Published in 1866 as the very best of contemporary Lancashire writing, this book now offers a wonderful insight into the cream of Lancashire literature in the middle of the last century. Nearly 150 years later, edited and republished, the book now presents a unique opportunity to read again the masters of our past.

ISBN 1 872226 50 7      £4.95

OTHER BOOKS TO LOOK OUT FOR BY
# PRINTWISE PUBLICATIONS LIMITED

## GREETINGS FROM NORTH WALES
(Cliff Hayes)
A personal view in over 100 postcards from 1890 to 1950
showing the North Wales that has enchanted so many visitors
ISBN 1 872226 44 2           £4.95

## GREETING FROM ECCLES
(Ted Gray)
Using over 100 postcards and archive photographs, local
historian Ted Gray follows the development of Eccles and
the surrounding area since 1892. Published in celebration of
the Centenary of the Eccles Charter
ISBN 1 872226 38 8           £4.95

## GREETINGS FROM THE WIRRAL
(Catherine Rothwell)
A portrait in old photographs and picture postcards
ISBN 1 872226 11 6           £4.95

## GREETINGS FROM OLD CHESHIRE
(Catherine Rothwell & Cliff Hayes)
A portrait in postcards and old photographs.
ISBN 1 872226 28 0           £4.95

## GREETINGS FROM THE LANCASHIRE COAST
(Catherine Rothwell and Cliff Hayes)
A pictorial history of the towns of the Lancashire coastline
captured in over 100 postcards
ISBN 1 872226 41 8           £4.95

# SONGS OF
# A Lancashire Warbler
by
Lowell Dobbs

Hoo seet mi heart gooin' back an' forrit,
   Thumpin' like a facthry mule-
Then hoo spun her charms areawnd it
   Like silk areawnd a spool.

£4.95

## look out for...

*Getting to Know...*
**THE RIBBLE VALLEY**

*Getting to Know...*
**PENDLE**

*Getting to Know...*
**THE LAKE DISTRICT**

RON & MARLENE FREETHY

price £4.95

# A MUST FOR EVERY KITCHEN
## The History of Lancashire Cookery
## by
## Tom Bridge

The History of Lancashire Cookery

Tom Bridge

price £4.95